ARLINGTON SCIENCE FOCUS SCHOOL
1501 NORTH LINCOLN STREET
ARLINGTON, VIRGINIA 22201

MW01071203

YOUR
Health

Harcourt

Orlando • Austin • Chicago • New York • Toronto • London • San Diego

Visit *The Learning Site!*
www.harcourtschool.com

CONSULTING AUTHORS

Charlie Gibbons, Ed.D.
Associate Professor
Alabama State University
Health, Physical Education and Dance Department
Montgomery, Alabama; and
School Age Coordinator
Maxwell Air Force Base, Alabama

Jan Marie Ozias, Ph.D., R.N.
Director, Texas Diabetes Council; and
Consultant, School Health Programs
Austin, Texas

Carl Anthony Stockton, Ph.D.
Professor of Health Education and Department Chair
Department of Health, Physical Education, and Recreation
The University of North Carolina at Wilmington
Wilmington, North Carolina

Printed in the United States of America

ISBN 0-15-334301-X

3 4 5 6 7 8 9 10 048 10 09 08 07 06 05 04 03

Contents

Emotional,
Intellectual,
and Social
Health

Understanding Life Skills

Good health isn't just what you know. You also need skills. The Life Skills in *Your Health* will help you stay healthy.

🍎 Make Decisions

Every day you decide, or choose what to do. Decisions about your health are important. Learning to make good decisions will help you stay healthy.

Think about your choices.

◀ Rita feels tired. She can't decide whether to go right to bed or brush her teeth first. How can she make the best choice?

Steps for Making Decisions

1. Think before you choose.

2. Imagine what could happen with each choice.

3. Make the best choice.

4. Think about what happened.

🍎 Manage Stress

"I'm so stressed!" Maybe you or a parent said that today. Stress is tension in your body or your mind. Some stress is normal, but too much stress can harm your health. Use the tips below to manage stress.

▶ **Tony will play goal keeper for an important soccer game tomorrow. He is worried and feels nervous and scared. How can he manage his stress to get through the game?**

Steps for Managing Stress

1. Know how stress feels.

2. Think about ways to handle stress.

3. Take one step at a time.

4. Learn ways to relax.

Say No

People can pressure you to do what you really don't want to. Knowing how to say *no* to unsafe actions can keep you healthy.

◀ Marcella's friend wants her to try some candy. Marcella is allergic to nuts. She isn't supposed to eat any candy without permission. How can Marcella say *no*?

How to Say *No*

1. Say **no**, and tell why not.

2. Think about what could happen.

3. Suggest something else to do.

4. Say **no** again. Walk away if you must.

Communicate

Communicating is another word for "sharing information." You have ideas and feelings. You communicate them with others to meet your needs.

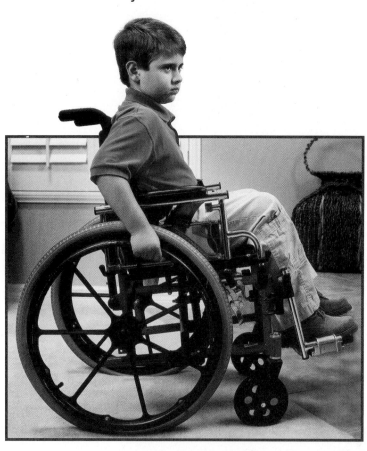

◀ There was a bad fire next door yesterday. David is scared, and he has questions about the fire. How can he communicate his feelings and needs to his family?

How to Communicate

1. Decide whom to talk to.

2. Say what you need to say.

3. Listen carefully, and answer any questions.

4. Get information.

...icts

...ient, is normal. However,

...to bad feelings or even a

...conflicts peacefully, it is better

◀ Jason wants to play the board game. Nina says she asked to play the game first. How can they resolve this conflict?

Steps for Resolving Conflicts

1. Agree that there is a problem.

2. Listen to each other.

3. Think of ways to work together.

4. Find a way for both sides to win.

Being a Wise Health Consumer

Being a wise consumer means making good bu decisions. You need to learn how ads can mislead y You also need to learn how to get good information about health.

▲ **Which of these soaps would you buy? Why?**

Make Buying Decisions

Advertising can help you make buying decisions. You should use oth information, too. Think carefully abo your needs. Use product information wisely to get the most for your money.

Steps for Making Buying Decisions

1. Decide if the item is a need, a want, or not important.

2. Compare several brands.

3. Choose the cheapest item that meets your needs.

4. Think about your buying choice.

Resolve

Conflict, or disag
big conflicts may le
fight. If you resolve
for everyone.

ıying

you.

ıer

ut

Analyze Advertising and Media Messages

Advertising is everywhere. Ads can give you good information about a product. They also can trick you. For example, an ad may suggest that a product will make you popular.

How to Analyze Advertising and Media Messages

1. Find out who made the message and why.

2. Watch for tricks. They can make you notice or agree with the message.

3. Notice the point of view shown.

4. Learn whether anything is left out.

Find Good Health Information

It's important to know facts about your health. Nurses, doctors, and pharmacists are reliable sources. Always think about the source of the information.

Find Good Health Information

1. Notice who said it. Are they selling anything?

2. Ask yourself if the information makes sense.

3. Ask yourself whether other sources agree.

4. Talk about it with your parents or another trusted adult.

You will learn and practice these important life skills as you use *Your Health.*

The Amazing Human Body

Getting enough rest, eating right, and staying active are the first steps to a healthful life.

Sense Organs

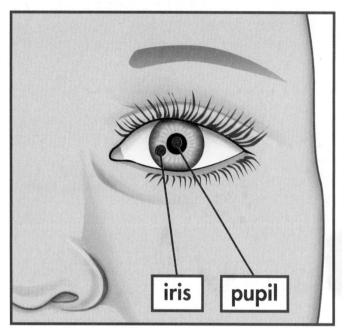

Outside of Eye

Caring for Your Eyes and Ears

- Sunglasses protect your eyes. Wear sunglasses when you are outdoors in sunlight or snow or on the water.
- Never put anything in your ears.

Eyes

Your eyes let you see. When you look at your eyes, you see a white part, a colored part, and a hole. The colored part is the iris. The hole in the middle is the pupil.

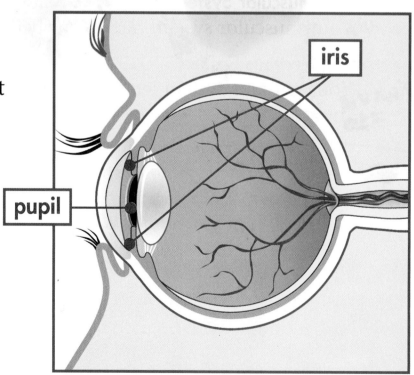

Inside of Eye

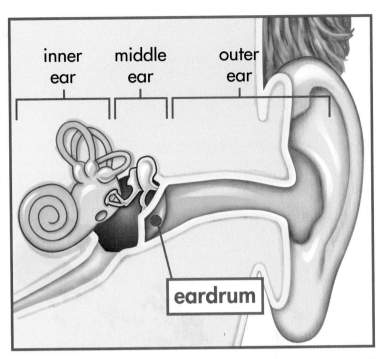

inner ear   middle ear   outer ear

eardrum

Inside of Ear   **Outside of Ear**

Ears

Your ears let you hear. What you see on the outside of your head is only part of your ear. The main part of your ear is inside your head.

ACTIVITIES

1. Put your hand over one eye for thirty seconds. Look in a mirror and take your hand away from your eye. What happens to the pupil of that eye?

2. Put a blindfold over your eyes and then cover one ear with your hand. Ask a classmate to stand somewhere in the room and clap. Point to where the sound came from. Are you pointing in the right direction?

The Skeletal System

Inside your body are hard, strong bones. These bones all fit together to make your skeleton. Your skeleton holds you up. Your bones help you move. Some of your bones protect parts of your body.

Caring for Your Skeletal System

- Exercise helps keep your bones strong.
- Wear a helmet and pads when you play sports.

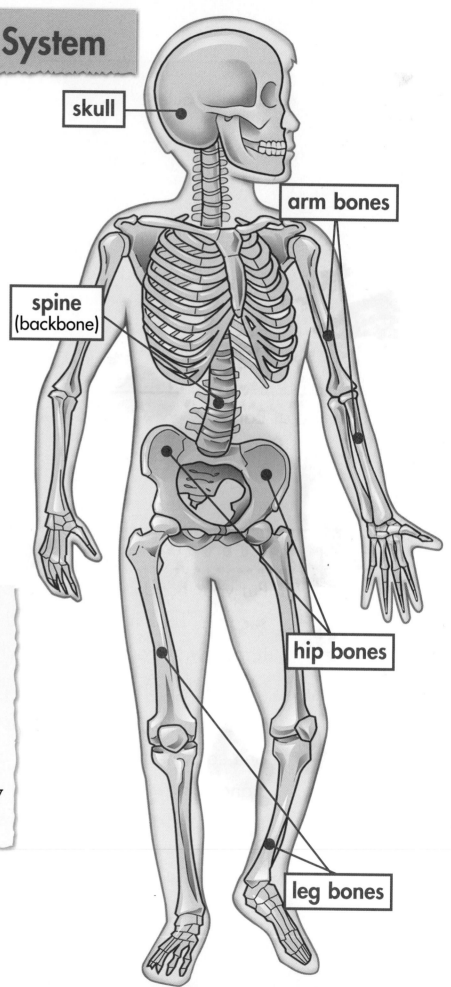

skull

arm bones

spine (backbone)

hip bones

leg bones

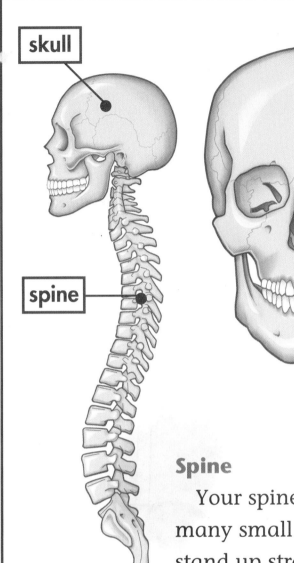

skull

spine

Skull

The bones in your head are called your skull. Some of the bones in your skull protect your brain. The bones in your face are part of your skull too.

Spine

Your spine, or backbone, is made up of many small bones. Your spine helps you stand up straight.

ACTIVITIES

1. Look at the picture of the skeleton. Do you have more bones in your legs or in your feet?

2. Have someone in your home measure your height before you go to bed at night. Get measured again when you wake up. Are you taller at night or in the morning?

The Digestive System

Your body gets good things from food. Your digestive system helps your body get energy from the food you eat. It helps your body get rid of the parts of the food it doesn't need to keep.

Caring for Your Digestive System

- Brush your teeth after every meal and before bedtime. Floss your teeth every day.

- Eat your food slowly. Chew your food well before you swallow it.

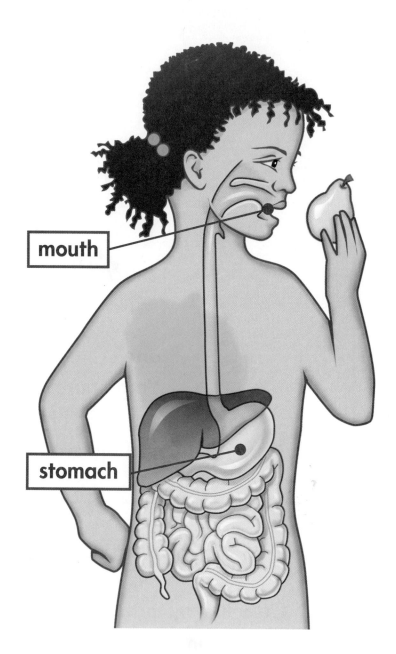

mouth

stomach

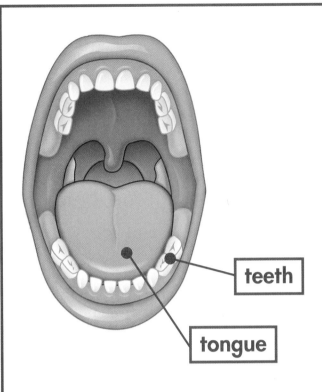

Mouth

You use different parts of your mouth when you eat. Your teeth chew the food. Your tongue tastes the food and pushes the food around your mouth and into your throat.

teeth

tongue

Stomach

Muscles in your stomach squeeze the food you eat. Juices in your stomach turn the food into a thick liquid.

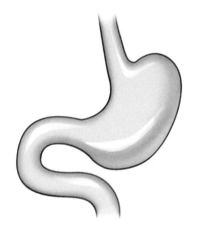

ACTIVITIES

1. Bite into an apple with your front teeth. Now chew with your front teeth. Which job is easier?

2. Have an adult help you fill a locking plastic bag with crackers and water. Lock the bag. Slowly mash the bag. This is how the muscles in the walls of your stomach mash the food you eat.

The Circulatory System

Blood goes through your body in your circulatory system. Your heart pumps the blood. Your blood vessels carry the blood.

Caring for Your Circulatory System

- Eat meat and green leafy vegetables. These foods give your blood iron. Iron in your blood carries oxygen.

- Keep germs out of your blood. When you get a cut, wash the skin around it with soap and water. Dry it carefully. Sometimes you need an antiseptic medicine to kill germs that are still there. Cover the cut with a bandage. Never touch someone else's blood.

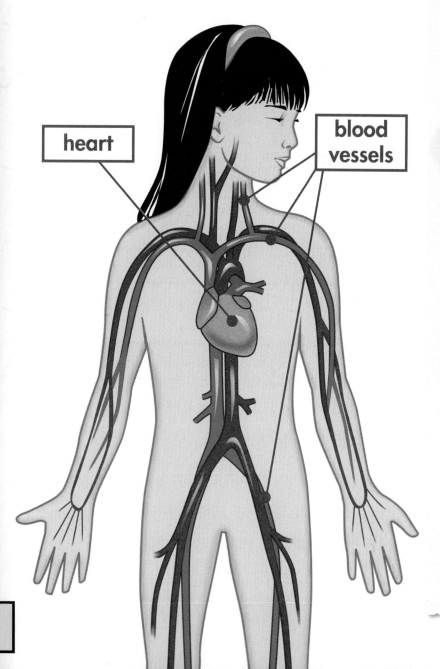

heart

blood vessels

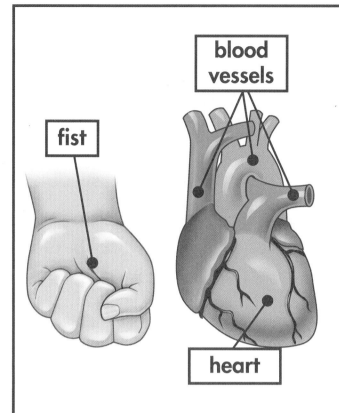

fist

blood vessels

heart

Heart

Your heartbeat is the sound of your heart pumping. When your heart pumps, it pushes blood through your body. Your heart pumps every second of every day. It is about the same size as your fist.

Blood Vessels

Blood vessels are tubes that carry blood through your body. Some blood vessels carry blood to your heart. Other blood vessels carry blood away from your heart.

ACTIVITIES

1. Get a small bucket of water. Make a fist and put it in the water. Squeeze your fist shut tightly. What happens to the water? This is how your heart pumps blood to all parts of your body.

2. Put your ear to a classmate's chest and listen to his or her heartbeat. Tell your classmate to jump up and down ten times. Listen again. What happens?

The Respiratory System

When you breathe, you are using your respiratory system. Your mouth, your nose, your lungs, and your diaphragm are parts of your respiratory system.

Caring for Your Respiratory System

- Never put anything in your nose.

- Playing helps your lungs. When you climb and jump, you breathe harder. Breathing harder makes your lungs stronger.

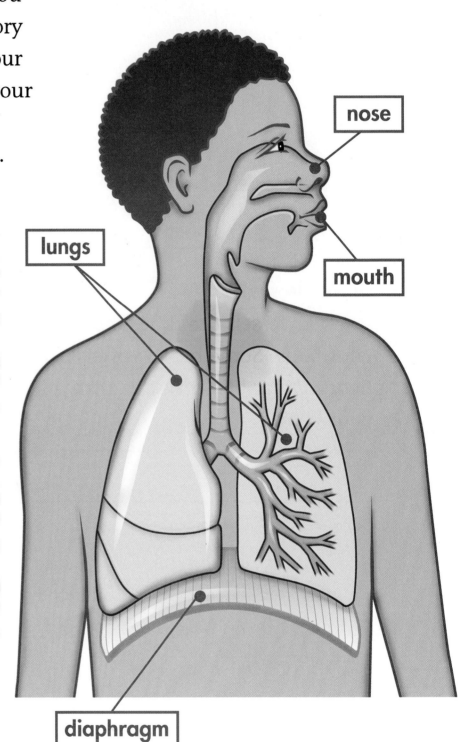

nose

mouth

lungs

diaphragm

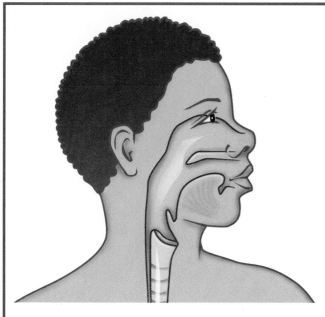

Mouth and Nose

Air goes in and out of your body through your mouth and nose. Your mouth and nose warm the air you breathe.

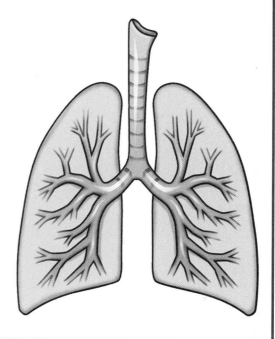

Lungs

You have two lungs. Your lungs are in your chest. When you breathe in, your lungs fill with air. When you breathe out, air leaves your lungs.

ACTIVITIES

1. Try to say something while you're breathing in. Try to say something while you're breathing out. Which is easier?

2. Breathe onto a mirror. What happens? Rinse your mouth with cold water. Again breathe on the mirror. What happens?

The Muscular System

The muscles in your body help you move. When you blink, you are using muscles. When you run, you are using muscles. Even when you eat, you are using muscles.

Caring for Your Muscular System
Stretch your muscles before you use them for play or exercise.

ACTIVITY ~
Wiggle your nose. Stick out your tongue. Wrinkle your forehead. Smile. Are you using muscles?

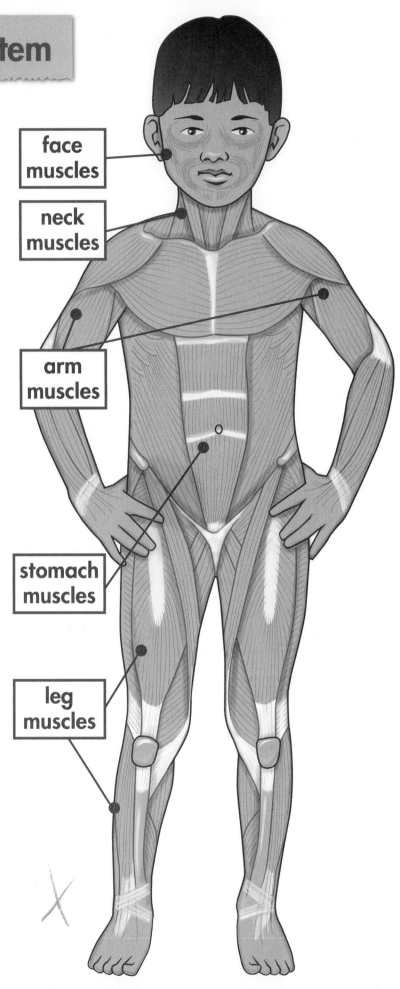

face muscles

neck muscles

arm muscles

stomach muscles

leg muscles

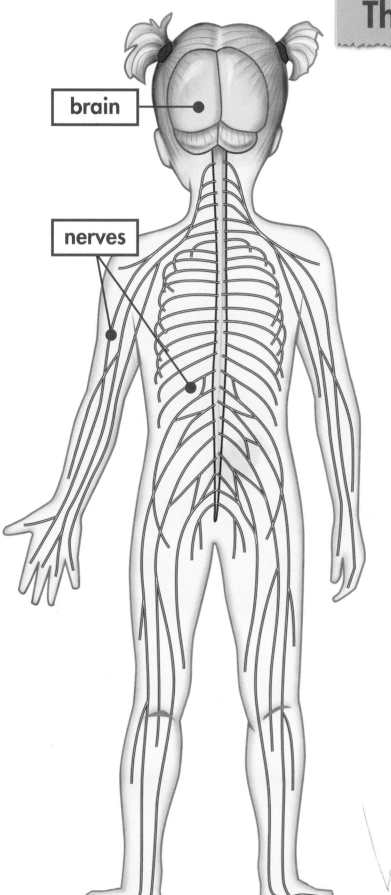

brain

nerves

Your nervous system makes your muscles work and tells you about your surroundings. Your brain and your nerves are parts of your nervous system.

Caring for Your Nervous System

Get plenty of sleep. Sleeping lets your brain rest.

ACTIVITY

Have a classmate blindfold you and fill one cup with cold water and another cup with warm water. Stick your finger in each cup. Can you tell which is the cold water and which is the warm water?

 1

My Feelings

 Project

Getting to Know You Make a book about yourself. Tell about your favorite things. Draw pictures of what you like to do. Tell about your friends.

For more things to do, visit the Internet.
www.harcourtschool.com

What makes people special?

You are **special**. No one else in the world is like you. No two people are exactly alike. Even twins who look alike are two **different** people.

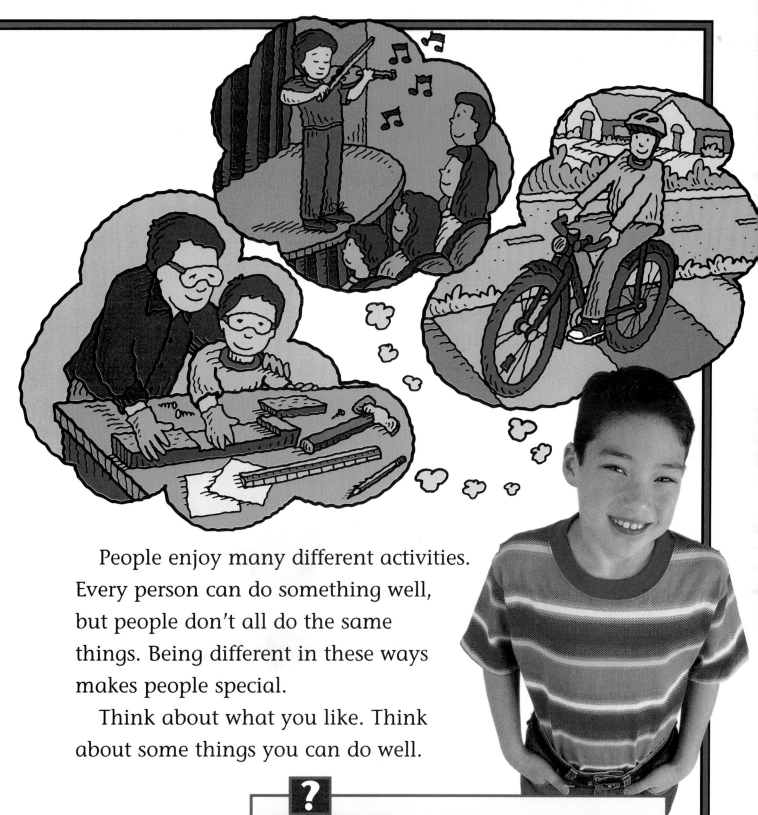

People enjoy many different activities. Every person can do something well, but people don't all do the same things. Being different in these ways makes people special.

Think about what you like. Think about some things you can do well.

?

CHECK

What is something that makes you special?

What feelings do I have?

You have many different **feelings** in the same day. At one time you may feel happy or sad. At another time you may feel angry.

People have all kinds of feelings. Your feelings are important.

Think about the feelings you have. How do you act when you have different feelings? When you are happy, you may smile or laugh. When you are sad, you may cry.

How do you act when you feel angry? If you harm someone or something, it will not help you feel better. Think of a way to act that will help. Talking about how you feel may help.

I feel like singing!

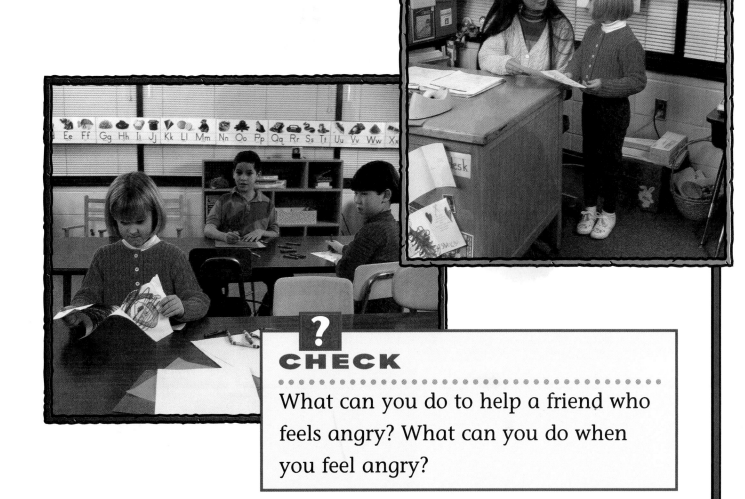

?

CHECK

What can you do to help a friend who feels angry? What can you do when you feel angry?

3

What helps when I feel worried or afraid?

Luis felt worried about his first day at a new school. He was afraid. Then Luis talked to his teacher. He met some new friends on the playground. Luis felt better.

Being **worried** is feeling troubled about something. Being **afraid** is feeling frightened. Everyone feels worried or afraid sometimes.

It is OK to be worried or afraid, but it does not feel good. When you feel worried or afraid, think about what you can do to feel better.

Talking about how you feel can help. Talk with a family member, a teacher, or a friend if you feel afraid or worried.

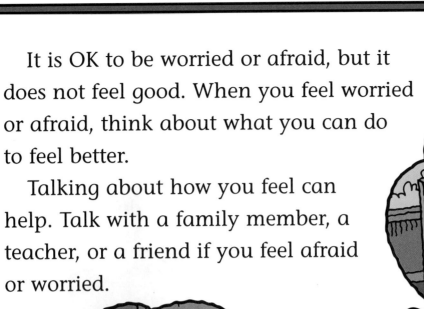

?

CHECK

Pretend Luis came to your school. What could you say or do to make him feel better?

MANAGE STRESS

Matt wakes up in the middle of the night. He sees shadows on his window and hears noises. Matt feels afraid. His fear causes **stress**. What should Matt do?

Learn This Skill

1. Know what stress feels like and what causes it.

Matt is scared. He is afraid to move. His muscles feel so tight he can hardly breathe.

2. When you feel stress, think about ways to handle it.

"I could call my parents to come help me."

"I could run into my parents' room."

"I could hide under my bed."

Matt can't just lie there. He has to do something.

3. Focus on one step at a time.

"Mom, Dad, I need you!"

Matt decides to call for his parents.

4. Learn to reduce tension.

Matt did the right thing. He asked for help from his parents when he was afraid.

Practice This Skill

Use the steps to help solve these problems.

A. Bo is shopping with his mother. He walks down an aisle to look at some games. When he looks up, he cannot find his mother. Bo is scared. What should he do?

B. Karla has a big karate match today. Her family is getting ready to go, but her brother is taking too long. Karla starts to worry that she will be late for her match. What should Karla do?

What helps when I make a mistake?

Have you ever spilled a drink or stepped on someone's toes? It is no fun to make a mistake!

All people make mistakes. When you make a mistake, you do not mean to do something wrong. There is nothing wrong with making a mistake. Mistakes can even help people learn how to do things the right way.

A mistake can cause harm, even though you did not do it on purpose. One thing you can do when you make a mistake is apologize. When you **apologize**, you say you are sorry. You make others feel better. You feel better too.

? CHECK

Why should you apologize when you make a mistake?

How can I respect others?

Getting along with others can be easy. One way to get along with others is to show respect. Showing **respect** means being thoughtful in what you say and do.

▲ Show respect in how you act.

▲ Show respect in how you talk.

◀ Show respect in how you touch.

Be polite to others. You are **polite** when
you say "Please" and "Thank you." You are
polite when you take turns.

? CHECK

Name three ways to show respect and
be polite.

How can I make a friend?

Having a friend makes you feel special. A **friend** is someone you like and trust. Think of all the things you can do with friends.

We have fun.

We can ride our bikes.

We can share lunch.

We can play together.

We can study together.

28

Treat your friends the way you want them to treat you. You are a good friend when you help others and show respect.

You can make new friends too. Invite someone new to play a game or sit with you at lunch. Find out what your new friend likes. Find out what your friend does well.

? CHECK

Make a list of words that describe a good friend.

Review

Use Health Words

special	different	feelings	worried
afraid	stress	apologize	respect
polite	friend		

Finish the sentences.

1. When you are troubled about something, you feel ___.

2. Every person, even a twin, is ___ from every other person.

3. If you make a mistake and hurt someone, you should ___, or say you are sorry.

4. Being thoughtful in what you say and do is showing ___.

5. You are ___. No one else is like you.

6. Happiness, sadness, and anger are kinds of ___.

7. Saying "Thank you" is a way to be ___.

8. Someone you like and trust is your ___.

9. When something frightens you, you feel ___.

10. Fear may cause ___.

Use Health Ideas

Answer the question.

11. Tell which children are showing respect.

Use Life Skills

Answer the question.

12. You are going to try out for a sports team for the first time. You are worried that you won't make the team. Tell what you can do to manage your stress.

Activities

- **On Your Own** Write a recipe for friendship. List what people should do to be a friend and to have friends.

- **With a Team** Make masks to show different kinds of feelings. Then act out stories about people who have these feelings.

My Family

Project

Family Favorites

Ask members of your family to tell you their favorite foods, games, and vacation places. Make a chart of their answers.

For more things to do, visit the Internet.
www.harcourtschool.com

How am I growing?

You are growing. **Growing** means you are getting bigger. You are getting older.

Think about what you looked like when you were a baby. Think about what you looked like in kindergarten. How have you changed?

1 year old

6 years old

10 years old

15
years old

30
years old

You will continue to grow. Once you were
a baby. Now you are a child. You will grow
to be a teenager. Later you will be an adult.

Growing means lots of changes. But no
matter how big you grow or how old you
are, you will still be you.

Everybody grows!

? CHECK

Name one thing you can do now that
you could not do when you were a baby.

How can my senses help me grow?

Senses help people grow, learn, and stay safe. Your **senses** are sight, hearing, smell, taste, and touch. You use your senses in many ways.

One important way you use your senses is for safety. **Safety** is keeping away from danger and not getting hurt.

You can use touch to tell whether something is too hot. You can use hearing to tell that a fast car is coming around the corner.

When you use your senses to stay safe, you can grow and be well.

? CHECK

How can you use your senses to learn things?

3

How do I grow in other ways?

Part of growing is learning to do new things. You learned to read. You learned to tie your shoes. Every day you learn something new.

Another part of growing is learning to be responsible. When you are **responsible**, you take care of things that should be done. You do not need to be told over and over what to do.

Following rules is being responsible. Taking care of your pet and cleaning your room are ways you show that you are responsible. As you grow, people will trust you to be more and more responsible.

? CHECK

What is one thing you are responsible for now?

How does my family help me grow?

Your family helps you grow. In a **family** people care about one another. Moms, dads, sisters, brothers, and grandparents are all family members.

Your family helps you grow by taking care of you. Family members can help you. They can show you how to grow, stay safe, and be responsible.

Every family is special. Every family is made up of people who are growing and learning.

? **CHECK**

Name one way your family helps you grow.

How can I help my family?

Your family helps you. You can help your family too.

One way to help is to do your share of work at home. You may have chores. **Chores** are special jobs you are responsible for doing to help your family.

How can I get along with family members?

Family members love one another. **Love** is a special feeling of caring for someone. Getting along with others in your family is one way to show love.

You get along with family members the same way you get along with other people. You show respect. You are polite.

Family members get along when they
work together to solve problems. They get
along when they listen to one another.
When family members get along, they grow
in love and respect.

?

CHECK

Tell how the family members in
the pictures are showing they love
one another.

45

RESOLVE CONFLICTS
in the Family

Zack shares a room with his brother. Zack likes everything to be neat. His brother always messes things up. Zack and his brother have a conflict. A **conflict** is a fight or a disagreement. Let's see how Zack and his brother can **resolve**, or settle, their conflict.

Learn This Skill

1. Stop.

Zack knows fighting will not help.

2. Agree to disagree.

Zack understands that his brother doesn't want to keep the room neat.

3. Talk about a solution.

Zack and his brother look around the room. They try to find a way to work out this problem.

4. Find a way for both sides to win.

We'll divide the room.

Then we can each have it the way we like it.

Zack and his brother make a deal.

Practice This Skill

Use the steps to help solve these problems.

A. Connie's family is baking. Connie wants a cake, and her brother wants cupcakes. How can they resolve this conflict?

B. Justin wants to wear his new shoes to school today. His parents want him to save them for a party this weekend. How can they resolve this conflict?

7

What does my family teach me?

Each family has its own way of doing things. Different families have their own ways to show love and respect. Each family has its own rules.

Your family can teach you many things. Older members teach younger members. Younger members can teach too. Talk with your family. Your family is an important part of your life.

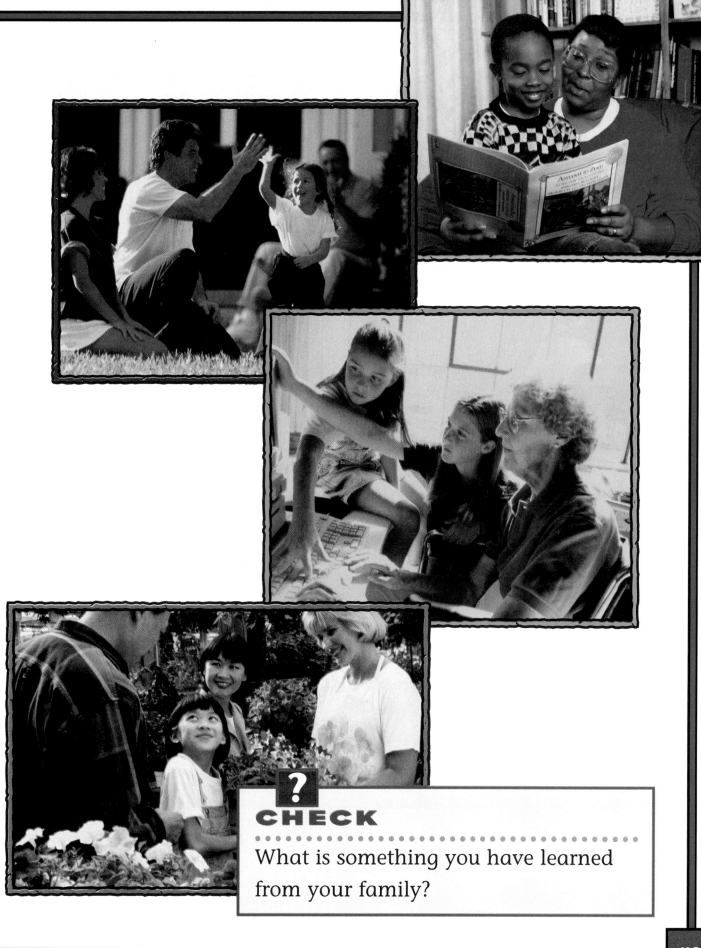

? CHECK

. . . .

What is something you have learned
from your family?

Review

Use Health Words

growing	senses	safety
responsible	family	chores
love	conflict	resolve

Finish the sentences.

1. When you take care of things that need to be done, you are being ___.

2. Another name for a disagreement or a fight is a ___.

3. You are getting bigger because you are ___.

4. Sisters and brothers are members of a ___.

5. Special jobs you are responsible for doing are your ___.

6. You can learn how to settle, or ___, conflicts.

7. Sight, hearing, smell, taste, and touch are your ___.

8. When you avoid danger, you are practicing ___.

9. A special feeling of caring for someone is called ___.

Use Health Ideas

Answer the questions.

10. List three ways you can help your family.

11. Tell how the children in the picture are using their senses.

Use Life Skills

Use what you know about resolving conflicts to solve this problem.

12. You just finished building a model city. Your little brother wants to knock it down. You tell him to stop, but he doesn't listen. What can you do?

Activities

- **On Your Own** Decorate place mats for your family members to use at a family meal. Make each person's place mat different and special.

- **With a Partner** Choose one of the senses. Make a poster showing how people can use that sense to learn, to enjoy things, and to stay safe.

Caring for My Teeth

FLOSS

What are the parts of a tooth?

There is more to your teeth than you can see. When you look at your teeth in a mirror, the part of each tooth you see is called the **crown**. You use the crowns of your teeth to help you bite or chew food.

Most of a tooth is hidden under the **gum**. The hidden part of a tooth is called the **root**. The roots hold your teeth in place.

The outside of a tooth is covered with **enamel**. Enamel is very hard. The inside of a tooth is much softer than the outside. The softest part is the **pulp** at the center of the tooth. The layer of tooth between the pulp and the enamel is called **dentin**.

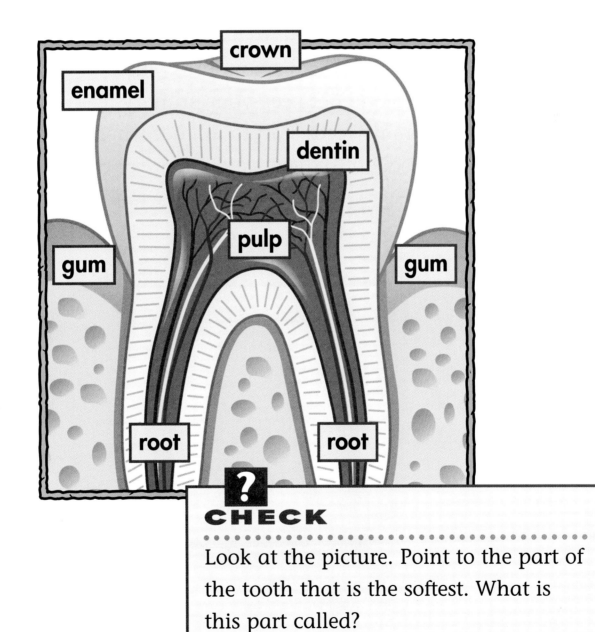

crown

enamel

dentin

pulp

gum

gum

root

root

?

CHECK

Look at the picture. Point to the part of the tooth that is the softest. What is this part called?

When do I get new teeth?

You will have two sets of teeth in your life. The first set are called **primary teeth**. There are 20 primary teeth in all. Your primary teeth started coming in when you were about six months old.

You do not keep your primary teeth. Primary teeth start to fall out when people are about six years old. They fall out to make room for a new set of teeth.

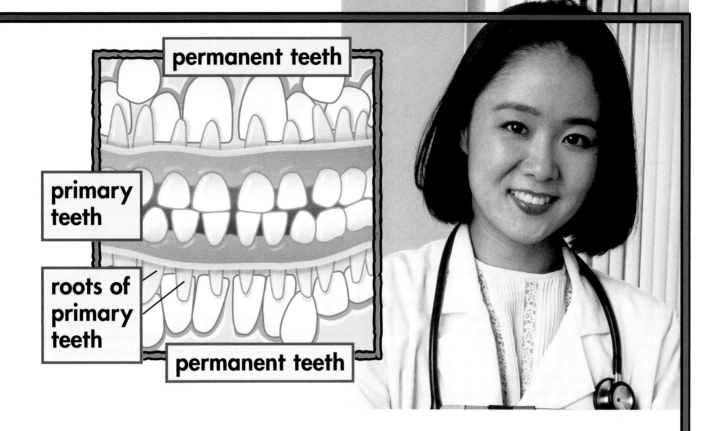

permanent teeth

primary teeth

roots of primary teeth

permanent teeth

Your second set of teeth are called **permanent teeth**. Permanent teeth begin coming in when people are five, six, or seven years old.

You will continue to get permanent teeth all through your childhood. By the time you are a young adult, you should have all 32 permanent teeth.

? CHECK

How many permanent teeth do you have now? How many more will you get?

How should I care for my teeth?

You can help keep your teeth healthy. One good way to care for your teeth is to keep them clean. Brush your teeth at least twice a day. Brush once in the morning after you eat breakfast. Brush again before you go to bed at night.

The pictures show how to brush the right way.

◀ **1. Brush the front sides of your teeth first. Move your toothbrush gently up and down.**

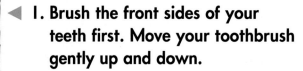

◀ **2. Then open your mouth, and brush the back side of each tooth.**

▼ **3. Brush the tops of your teeth last.**

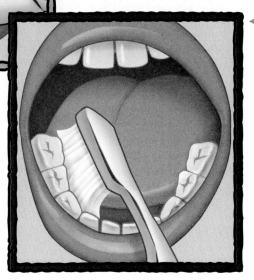

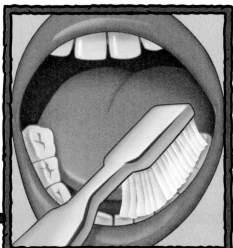

You also need to clean between your teeth once a day. Use a special thread called **floss**. Bedtime is the best time to use floss. Ask an adult to watch you floss so that you do it the right way.

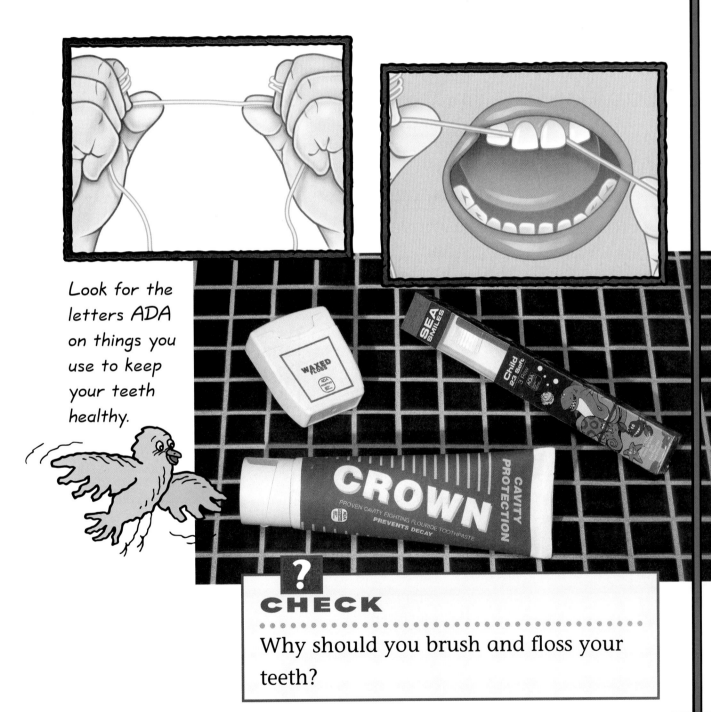

Look for the letters ADA on things you use to keep your teeth healthy.

?
CHECK
• •
Why should you brush and floss your teeth?

What foods help keep my teeth healthy?

Eating the right kinds of foods is another way to keep your teeth healthy. The pictures show the kinds of foods you should eat every day.

Be sure to eat enough foods from the milk, yogurt, and cheese group each day. These foods have lots of calcium. **Calcium** helps your teeth grow strong.

milk, cheese, yogurt

meat, poultry, fish, dried beans, eggs, nuts

vegetables

fruits

▲ If you get hungry between meals, try a snack of fresh vegetables. Foods from the vegetable group have little sugar.

You may eat a small amount of sweets sometimes. Try to eat sweets only with a meal that includes other foods. Brush your teeth after you eat sweets.

Most foods have some sugar in them. Sugar can harm your teeth if it stays on them too long. Brushing helps clean the sugar from your teeth.

bread, cereal, rice, pasta

? CHECK

Make a list of five things you like to eat. Put a star next to the foods that are good for your teeth.

MAKE DECISIONS
About Your Teeth

Making good choices about food helps keep your teeth healthy. Ruth goes to the grocery store with her father. Her father asks her to get the orange juice. How can Ruth choose which orange juice they should buy?

Learn This Skill

1. Think before you choose.

Ruth looks at the containers. There is regular orange juice and orange juice with calcium.

2. Imagine what could happen with each choice.

Ruth knows that both kinds of orange juice taste good. She knows that calcium is good for her teeth and bones.

3. Make the best choice.

Ruth chooses the orange juice with calcium.

4. Think about what happened.

Ruth has a drink that tastes good and helps keep her teeth healthy.

Practice This Skill

Use the steps to help you solve the problems below.

A. You go to the store with your family. You need toothpaste. Use the decision-making steps to choose what kind to buy.

B. You can choose an apple, a glass of milk, or a candy bar as a snack. Use what you know about making decisions and keeping your teeth healthy to choose a snack.

What happens when I get a cavity?

If you eat sweets and starches too often, you can get a cavity. A **cavity** is a hole in a tooth. You can also get a cavity from not brushing and flossing your teeth often enough.

If you get a cavity in your tooth, you need to see a dentist. You should see your dentist for regular checkups.

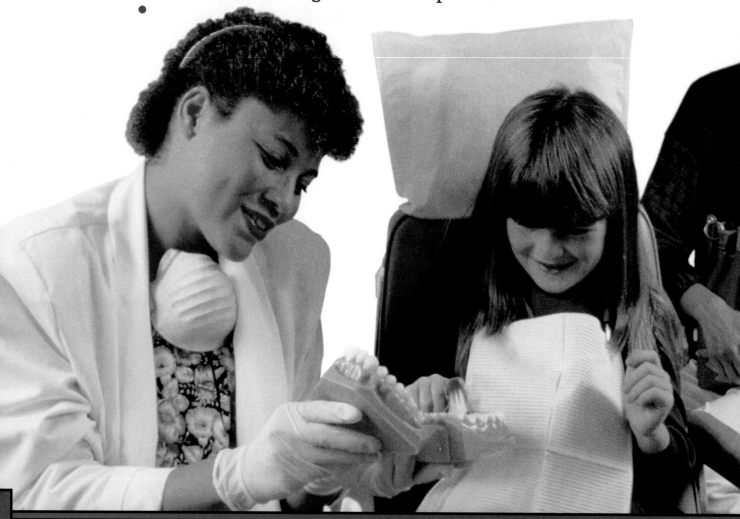

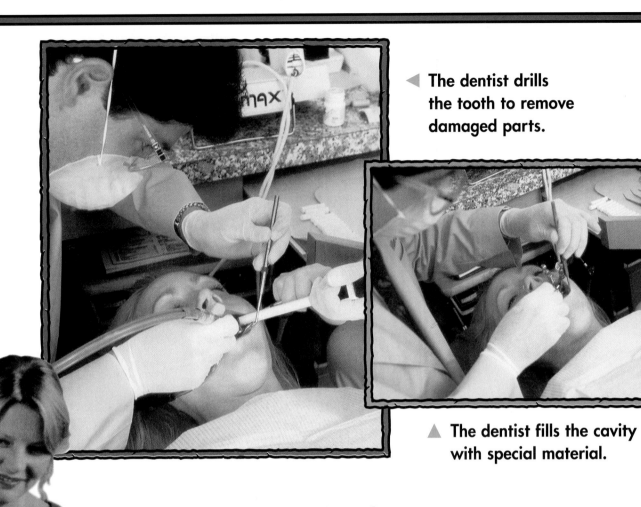

◀ The dentist drills the tooth to remove damaged parts.

▲ The dentist fills the cavity with special material.

The pictures show how a dentist fixes a cavity.

Dentists and dental hygienists help you keep your teeth healthy, too. They teach you how to care for your teeth. They help you learn how to brush and floss the right way.

? CHECK

How does a dentist fix a cavity?

Review

Use Health Words

crown	gum	root
enamel	pulp	dentin
primary teeth	permanent teeth	floss
calcium	cavity	

Finish the sentences.

1. To keep your teeth healthy, you should brush and ___ every day.

2. Your first set of teeth are called the ___.

3. The part of the tooth you can see in a mirror is called the ___.

4. The hardest part of the tooth is the ___.

5. Your second set of teeth are called the ___.

6. To help your teeth grow strong, eat foods that have ___.

7. When you look in a mirror, the root of a tooth is hidden by the ___.

8. A hole in a tooth is called a ___.

9. The softest part of the tooth is the ___.

10. The part of the tooth that is under the gum is the ___.

11. The layer of tooth between the enamel and the pulp is called ___.

Use Health Ideas

Answer the questions.

12. Tell how to brush your teeth properly.

13. Tell how to floss your teeth properly.

14. What should you do if you get a cavity?

Use Life Skills

Use the picture to answer the question.

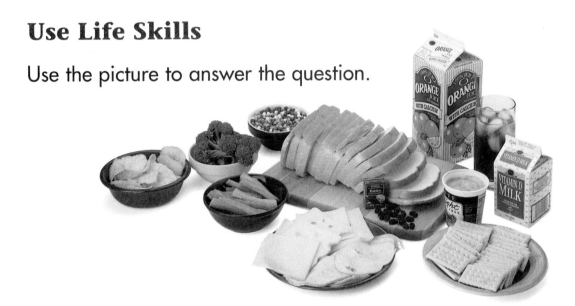

15. Which foods would you choose to make up a lunch that is good for your teeth? Tell why you chose as you did.

Activities

- **On Your Own** Write a story about a visit to the dentist. Draw pictures to go with your story.

- **With a Partner** Make a model of a tooth. Label the parts of the tooth.

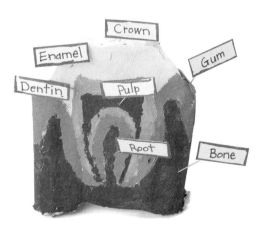

Keeping Fit and Healthy

For Our Health

Make a plan of healthful habits and activities for your class. Decorate a class calendar with your ideas for staying healthy.

For more things to do, visit the Internet.
www.harcourtschool.com

Why should I keep myself clean?

Germs! Germs! Germs! **Germs** may be too tiny to see, but they can make you ill. Keeping yourself clean helps remove germs.

Keep your body, hair, and nails clean by taking baths or showers. Wash your hands with soap and warm water to remove germs.

◄ Ah-choo! After you blow your nose or sneeze, always wash your hands.

▲ After you use the rest room, wash your hands for as long as it takes to say your ABCs.

◀ Before you eat, don't forget to wash your hands with soap!

◀ It's fun to play with pets, but animals carry germs. Don't forget to wash your hands after you touch an animal. And don't touch wild animals or animals you don't know at all!

? CHECK

How does keeping yourself clean help you stay healthy?

How should I care for my skin?

Keeping your skin clean is one way to stay healthy. But germs aren't the only thing that can harm your skin. You need to protect your skin from the sun, too.

Even on a cloudy day, you can get a sunburn. A **sunburn** is a burning of the skin by the sun's rays. A sunburn is painful. It can cause skin damage.

Sunscreen is a lotion that protects your skin from the sun's rays. You should wear sunscreen whenever you go outside.

On sunny days, protect your skin and eyes by wearing a hat and sunglasses.

? CHECK

Why should you protect yourself from the sun?

How should I care for my eyes?

Think of all the ways you use your eyes. Your sense of sight helps you learn about the world. It helps you enjoy things. Using your eyes can help keep you safe.

DON'T WALK

ST

You can protect your eyes in many ways. Never touch or rub your eyes with dirty hands. Be careful when you use sharp things. Wear special protection for your eyes when you play some sports.

Have your eyes checked to make sure they are working well. Wear glasses if you need them to see better.

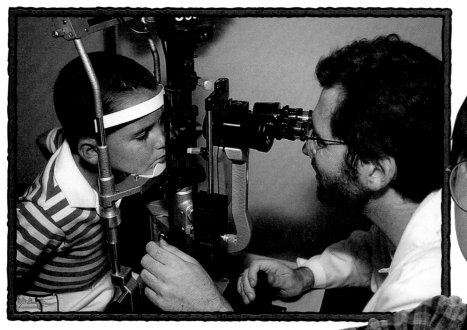

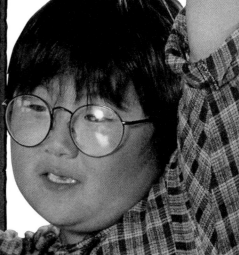

?

CHECK

Why should you take care of your eyes?

How should I take care of my ears?

You hear a funny joke and you laugh. You listen to your favorite music on the radio. You talk on the phone with a friend. You hear the sound of a fire engine siren, so you stop your bike by the curb.

Your ears are important. Your sense of hearing helps keep you safe. It also helps you enjoy things.

Take care of your ears. Then your ears can help take care of you!

- Never put anything in your ears.

- Keep your ears clean.

- Keep your ears warm in the winter.

- Stay away from loud noises. They can hurt your ears.

- Protect your ears from injury.

? CHECK

Name one way your ears can help keep you safe.

How can exercise keep me healthy?

Which activities do you like best? Soccer? Dancing? Swimming? Skating? Walking? Riding your bike?

All these activities are ways to exercise. **Exercise** is active use of your body. Exercise is fun and healthful. Exercise makes you fit. Being **fit** means being healthy and having lots of energy.

Exercise makes your heart, lungs, and muscles strong. It helps you fight germs and grow healthy. When you exercise, you feel and look good. You have lots of energy.

? CHECK

Look at the pictures. What are the children doing to keep their bodies strong and healthy?

Lesson 6

What are safe ways to exercise?

Exercise is good for you. Learning how to exercise the right way keeps you safe.

No matter what kind of exercise you do, follow the same four steps to stay safe.

▲ 1. Stretch!

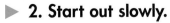

► 2. Start out slowly.

80

▲ 3. Speed up!

▶ 4. Cool down before
you stop.

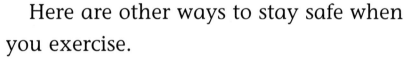

Here are other ways to stay safe when
you exercise.

- Wear the right kind of clothing and
  safety equipment.
- Drink lots of water because your body
  loses water when you sweat.
- Rest when you feel tired.
- Stop right away if you feel pain.

?
CHECK
Why do you think you should stretch
before you exercise?

MANAGE STRESS
with Exercise

Kaley's grandparents are coming to visit. Kaley is so excited. She just can't wait. Kaley feels stress. How can she manage her stress?

Learn This Skill

1. Know how stress feels.

Kaley feels she can't sit still.

2. Think about ways to handle stress.

Kaley doesn't want to sit around waiting for another hour.

3. Take one step at a time.

Kaley thinks of a way to make the time go faster.

4. Learn ways to relax.

Exercise helped Kaley relax while she waited for her grandparents.

Practice This Skill

Use the steps to help you solve the problems below.

A. Luke is going to a new dentist for his checkup. He feels nervous. How can Luke manage his stress?

B. Kristen is worried about taking a special test. How can she manage her stress?

How does sleep help me stay healthy?

"Just let me stay up for five more minutes!"

You may have said those words. Maybe you wanted to read one more chapter of a book. Maybe you just didn't feel sleepy.

But think of how you feel when you don't get enough sleep. On those mornings you probably say, "Let me have just five more minutes to sleep!"

Your body needs sleep to stay healthy. When you sleep, your body works to fight germs and keep you from becoming ill. Sleep gives your body energy to run and play.

When you have enough sleep, you can learn more easily. When you are rested, you feel better.

?

CHECK

What does your body do while you are sleeping?

Review

Use Health Words

germs   sunburn   sunscreen
exercise   fit

Finish the sentences.

1. When you are healthy and have lots of energy, you feel ___.

2. Washing with soap and warm water helps remove ___ that can cause illness.

3. Even on cloudy days, you need to protect your skin with ___.

4. Active use of the body is called ___.

5. The sun's rays can damage your skin and give you a ___.

Use Health Ideas

Answer the questions.

6. List three ways you can take care of your eyes.

7. Why does your body need sleep?

8. What four steps should you follow any time you exercise?

9. Which child is doing something that can damage the ears?

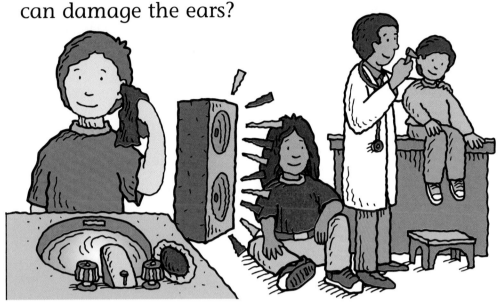

Use Life Skills

Use what you know about managing stress to solve this problem.

10. You are going to an overnight camp for the first time. You are excited and a little afraid. You have two hours before the bus picks you up. What can you do to help manage your stress?

Activities

- **On Your Own** Make or decorate a hat or visor to wear on sunny days.

- **With a Team** Learn a new playground game or other form of exercise. Teach it to your class.

Food for Fitness

Recipes for Health
Make a cookbook
of foods you like
to eat. Choose
recipes that you
think will make
healthful meals.

**For more things to do,
visit the Internet.**
www.harcourtschool.com

How does my body use food?

Whatever your body does, it uses energy. **Energy** is the power your body needs to move, stretch, blink, and breathe. You get energy from the food you eat.

Your body uses food to keep its parts working well. Your heart, skin, bones, and all your other body parts need food to stay healthy.

Your body uses food to help you grow. You may have grown an inch or more since last year.

Food also helps keep you healthy. It helps you get better if you are hurt.

No one food can do all these things for you. You must eat many kinds of food to get what your body needs.

? CHECK

Name two ways your body uses food.

Do I know what to eat?

Your body needs more of some kinds of food and less of other kinds of food. The **Food Guide Pyramid** shows which groups different foods belong to. It shows how many servings from each food group you should eat each day. A **serving** is the amount of food in one helping.

fats, sweets only small amounts

milk, yogurt, cheese 2–3 servings

vegetables 3–5 servings

bread, cereal, rice, pasta 6–11 servings

Eat more servings of foods from the bottom of the pyramid. Eat only small amounts of foods from the top of the pyramid.

The Food Guide Pyramid can help you decide what to eat. It can help you make healthful food choices.

meat, poultry, fish, dried beans, eggs, nuts
2–3 servings

fruits
2–4 servings

? CHECK

Use the Food Guide Pyramid to plan a healthful menu for one day's meals.

Do I get the water I need?

Water is very important to your health. Your body uses water for almost everything it does. Water helps keep your body at the right temperature. It helps break food down and move it to different parts of the body. Water helps your body get rid of **wastes**, or materials your body doesn't need.

You should drink six to eight glasses of water a day. When you exercise, you need to drink even more water.

You can get some of the water your body needs by drinking juices and milk. You can get water from some foods, such as fruits and vegetables. But drinking water often during the day is the best way to get what your body needs.

?
CHECK

How much water should you drink every day?

What makes a healthful lunch?

Eating three meals a day helps supply the energy your body needs. **Lunch** is the meal most people eat in the middle of the day.

During the week you probably eat lunch at school. What are some of the foods these children are choosing?

Some foods are more healthful than others. Foods that contain large amounts of fat, salt, or sugar do not make the best choices. **Fat** is the part of food that contains the most energy. Your body needs some fat, but too much fat is not healthful. The same is true for salt and sugar.

?

CHECK

How can you use the Food Guide Pyramid to help you choose a healthful lunch?

How should I shop for food?

Shopping is a good time to practice making healthful choices. You can use the Food Guide Pyramid to help you shop. Choose foods from all the food groups.

When you shop, you should read food labels. The label lists all the **ingredients** in the food. When you read the label, you can choose foods with healthful ingredients.

INGREDIENTS: CORN SYRUP, RICE FLOUR, SUGAR, ROLLED OATS, COCOA BUTTER, APPLES, DATES, CORN BRAN, BARLEY FLOUR, MILK, RICE BRAN, RASPBERRIES, CITRIC ACID, SUNFLOWER OIL, LECITHIN.

CHEWY GRANOLA BARS

Read the labels on cereal boxes carefully. Some cereals taste sweet because they are made with lots of sugar. Too much sugar is not good for you. Have an adult help you read cereal labels. If sugar appears near the top of the ingredients list, find a better choice.

Watch out for too much sugar!

?

CHECK

Why should you read food labels?

MAKE DECISIONS
About Snacks

Cole and his dad are going food shopping. Cole is looking for snacks that will taste good and be healthful.

Learn This Skill

1. Think before you choose.

There are so many snacks. Cole decides to compare the ingredients.

2. Imagine what could happen with each choice.

Cole likes both snacks. He thinks about which one to choose.

3. Make the best choice.

Cole reads that the candy bars have more sugar than the pretzels.

4. Think about what happened.

Cole enjoys the pretzels at snack time.

Practice This Skill

Use the steps to help you solve the problems below.

A. Michelle's family members take turns planning meals. Michelle gets to plan Sunday's dinner. Use what you know about the Food Guide Pyramid to help Michelle plan her meal.

B. Charlie's family is going for a long bicycle ride. They will be gone for several hours. They will each have a water bottle. Help Charlie decide what foods he can bring to get extra water.

Why is keeping clean at mealtimes important?

You know that germs can make you ill. One way germs get into your body is through your mouth when you eat. Keeping clean at mealtimes helps fight germs.

Make sure the food you eat is clean and not spoiled. Wash raw vegetables and fruits before you eat them. Never eat meat, poultry, or eggs that aren't cooked all the way. Don't eat or drink anything you find on the ground or in the trash.

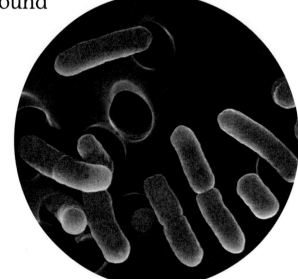

▲ This is what germs look like through a microscope. Germs like these can make you ill if they are in the foods you eat.

Wash your hands with soap and warm water before you eat or drink anything. Be sure the plate, bowl, glass, knife, fork, and spoon you use are also clean. Don't share cups, glasses, dishes, forks, or spoons with other people.

Keeping clean at mealtimes helps your body get the healthful food it needs.

?
CHECK

Why should you not share glasses or spoons with others?

Review

CHAPTER 5

Use Health Words

energy	Food Guide Pyramid	serving
wastes	lunch	fat
ingredients		

Finish the sentences.

1. The meal that most people eat in the middle of the day is ___.

2. You can find out about different food groups from the ___.

3. You should avoid snacks that have too much sugar, salt, or ___.

4. Water helps your body get rid of ___, or things your body doesn't need.

5. The power your body needs to do things is ___.

6. Read food labels to find whether the ___ are healthful.

7. The amount of food in one helping is called a ___.

Use Health Ideas

Answer the questions.

8. List three ways your body uses water.

9. For each picture, tell what the child is doing wrong. Tell how each child can stay safe from germs at mealtime.

Use Life Skills

Use the steps for making decisions to make a healthful food choice.

10. You are having lunch with your family in a restaurant. You can have vegetable pizza and a salad, a hot dog with chips, or fried chicken and french fries. Which lunch do you choose? Tell why.

Activities

- **On Your Own** Compare the labels of three cereals you like. Tell which cereal has the most healthful ingredients.

- **With a Partner** Make a poster of the Food Guide Pyramid. Put pictures of your favorite foods in the correct food groups.

Staying Well

Project

The Wellness Game Make up a board game about staying well. Let players move ahead when they make healthful choices.

For more things to do, visit the Internet.
www.harcourtschool.com

What is an illness?

When you are not well, you are **ill**. Parts of your body may hurt. You may have a fever. You may feel very tired.

An illness is a **disease**. Illnesses can be treated. You might need to stay home and rest when you are ill. Rest helps the body get better. You might visit a doctor or go to a clinic.

At home, tell your family if you feel ill. At school, tell your teacher if you don't feel well. Be sure to say which part of your body hurts, or whether you feel hot or tired.

? CHECK

Why do you think people who are ill should stay home and rest?

COMMUNICATE
When You Are Ill

Rachel feels sick at school. She feels hot and very weak. She just wants to put her head on her desk and sleep. Rachel knows she needs help.

Learn This Skill

1. Decide whom to talk to.

To whom should Rachel talk?

2. Say what you need to say.

I think I'm sick. My head hurts.

What can Rachel say?

3. Listen carefully, and answer any questions.

Do you feel hot?

Yes. And I'm very sleepy.

Rachel's teacher tries to find out more about how she is feeling.

4. Follow directions.

The nurse will decide if you need to go home. I hope you feel better tomorrow.

NURSE Station

Rachel follows her teacher's directions.

Practice This Skill

Use the steps to help you solve this problem.

Noah is spending the night at a friend's house. His stomach hurts. Who should he tell? What should he say about how he feels?

How is illness spread?

Some diseases are caused by germs. Germs can spread from person to person, carrying disease with them. A cold is a disease caused by germs. Chicken pox is another disease that can spread from person to person.

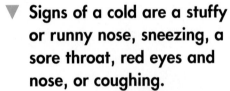

▼ Signs of a cold are a stuffy or runny nose, sneezing, a sore throat, red eyes and nose, or coughing.

▼ Signs of chicken pox are red bumps on the skin of the head, face, and body. The bumps become itchy blisters and then form crusty scabs.

There are things you can do to keep from spreading or catching germs.

- Wash your hands often.

- Keep your hands away from your nose, eyes, and mouth.

- Don't put objects in your mouth.

- Use a tissue when you sneeze, cough, or blow your nose. Then throw the tissue away, and wash your hands.

- Don't get close to people who have colds.

- Stay home when you have an illness that can be easily spread.

?

CHECK

Name two things to do if you are around someone who is coughing and sneezing.

How can we prevent illness?

You know there are ways to keep illness from spreading. But there is also a way to keep your body from ever getting some illnesses. You can get vaccines.

Vaccines help prevent some diseases. If you have had the vaccine for a disease, you should not become ill even if you catch the disease germs. The vaccine will help your body fight off the germs.

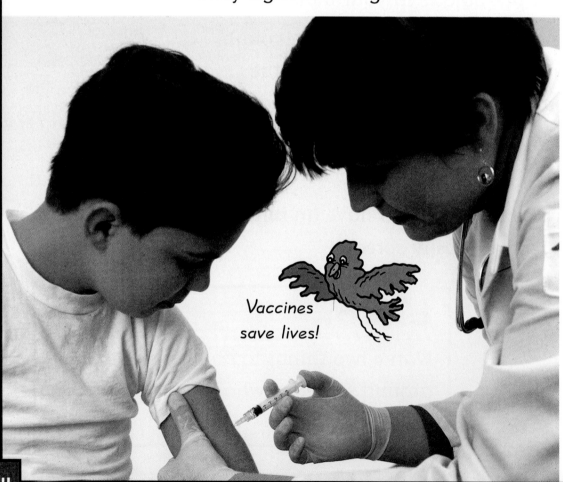

Vaccines save lives!

You can get vaccines to protect yourself against diseases such as measles, mumps, polio, and chicken pox. These diseases can make people very ill.

Most children start getting vaccines when they are babies. Most vaccines are given as shots. Vaccines help keep diseases from spreading.

? CHECK

Why should people get vaccines?

How are head lice spread?

Sometimes children get head lice. **Head lice** are tiny bugs that live on the scalp. They lay sticky eggs on hair. The bugs bite the skin and cause itching. When the skin is scratched, germs can cause sores.

Head lice can be easily passed from one person to another. To keep from getting head lice, follow these rules.

- Don't share brushes and combs.

- Don't wear someone else's hat, earphones, or helmet.

- Don't share clothes, pillows, or toys with someone who has head lice.

- Don't put heads together when talking or working with a friend.

Special shampoos can kill head lice and their eggs. The eggs must be pulled off or combed out. After a few days the itching will stop. Children with head lice should stay home until the head lice are gone, to keep from passing them to others.

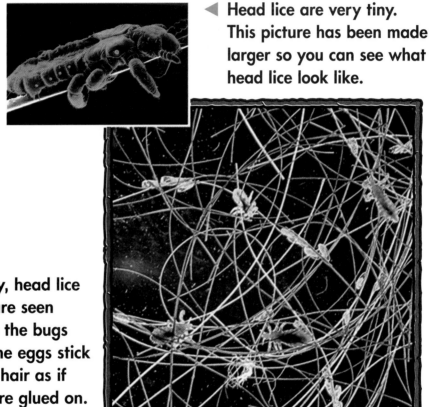

◄ Head lice are very tiny. This picture has been made larger so you can see what head lice look like.

► Usually, head lice eggs are seen before the bugs are. The eggs stick to the hair as if they are glued on.

CHECK

Why is it important not to wear someone else's hat or bicycle helmet?

What are some other kinds of illnesses?

Not all diseases are passed from one person to another. **Asthma** is an illness that makes it hard to breathe. If you have asthma, you may cough even though you do not have a cold.

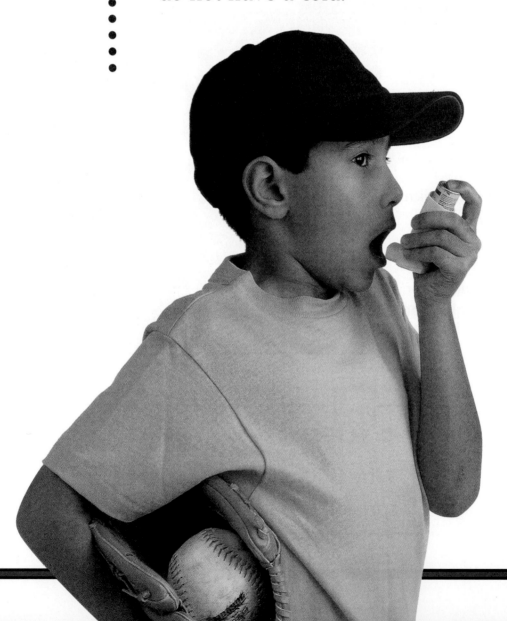

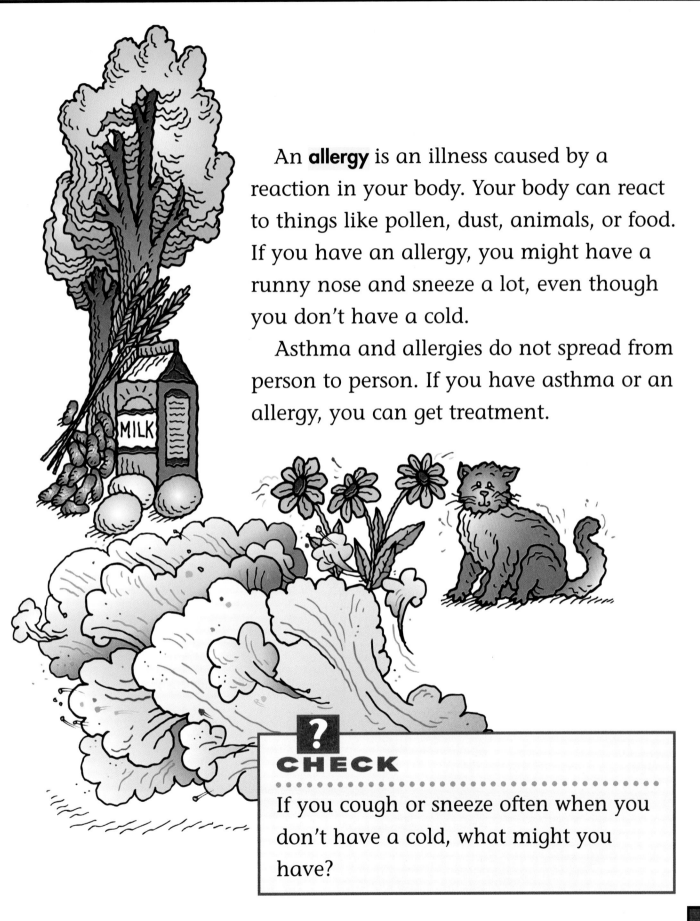

An **allergy** is an illness caused by a reaction in your body. Your body can react to things like pollen, dust, animals, or food. If you have an allergy, you might have a runny nose and sneeze a lot, even though you don't have a cold.

Asthma and allergies do not spread from person to person. If you have asthma or an allergy, you can get treatment.

? CHECK

If you cough or sneeze often when you don't have a cold, what might you have?

How can I stay well?

Think of all the people who help you take care of your body.

▼ Your family makes sure you get healthful food and plenty of sleep at night.

▲ A doctor can give you vaccines and treat you when you are ill.

◀ A school nurse can check to see that you are growing well. A nurse can help when you feel ill, too.

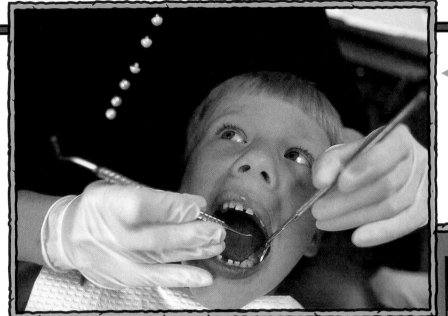

◄ A dentist can help fix any problems with your teeth and gums.

What important person is left out? You! You can help keep your body clean. You can eat and sleep well. You can get lots of exercise. Be sure to have fun, too. When you enjoy yourself, your whole body feels better.

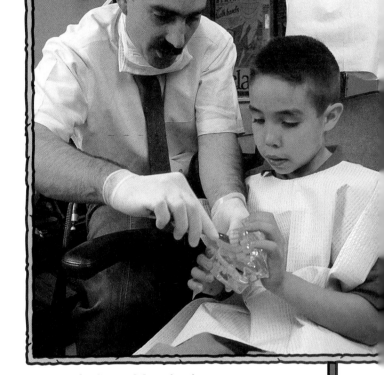

▲ A dental hygienist can help keep your teeth clean and healthy.

?
CHECK

Name three things you can do today to help keep yourself well.

Review

Use Health Words

ill	disease	vaccines
head lice	asthma	allergy

Finish the sentences.

1. When you are ill, you may have a ___, such as a cold or chicken pox.

2. Tiny bugs called ___ cause itching and can be spread easily.

3. When you are not feeling well, you are ___.

4. If you sneeze when you are around trees or flowers, you may have an ___ to pollen.

5. To keep from getting some diseases, you can get ___.

6. If you cough when you do not have a cold or an allergy, you may have ___.

Use Health Ideas

Answer the questions.

7. Tell how illnesses are spread from person to person.

8. Name three people who can help you stay well.

9. Look at the pictures. Tell how each thing can cause illness.

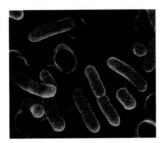  

Use Life Skills

Answer the question.

10. List four steps you should follow to communicate when you are ill.

Activities

- **On Your Own** Make a checklist of things you can do to stay well. Put a star next to each thing you do this week.

- **With a Team** Make up a play about going to the doctor to get a vaccine. Put on your play for younger children.

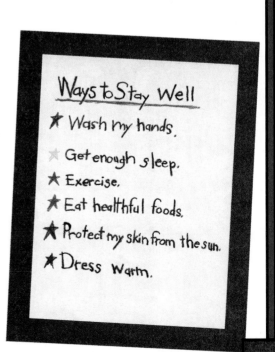

Ways to Stay Well
★ Wash my hands.
★ Get enough sleep.
★ Exercise.
★ Eat healthful foods.
★ Protect my skin from the sun.
★ Dress warm.

Medicines and Drugs

Project

The No Book
Make a book about ways to say no to drugs. Make sure your book also tells how to stay safe around medicines.

For more things to do, visit the Internet.
www.harcourtschool.com

What are medicines?

When you are ill or hurt, you may need medicines. **Medicines** are used to treat diseases and fight germs. Medicines can make people feel better when they have pain or a fever. Sometimes medicines are needed to help you stay well.

A medicine can be a liquid, powder, spray, cream, or pill. Look at the pictures. Who is giving medicine to help fight germs on the skin? Who is getting medicine to help fight germs inside the body?

? CHECK

How do medicines help people?

How can I use medicines safely?

Medicines must be used in the right way. Always have a trusted adult give you medicine.

All medicines come with **instructions**. The instructions are written on the label. The person who gives you medicine must read the label carefully.

Don't take medicine without an adult's help.

INSTRUCTIONS:
- Take one tablet three times a day.
- Take with milk or food.
- Do not mix with other medicines.

All medicines should be kept in a locked
cabinet. Never take someone else's medicine.
A medicine that can help one person may
not be good for someone else.

?

CHECK

List three rules for using medicines
safely.

What are drugs?

A medicine is a kind of drug. **Drugs** change the way the body works. When medicines are used safely, they help the body fight illnesses.

Some drugs are not medicines. These drugs can harm the body. Beer, wine, and liquor are drinks that contain a drug. Cigarettes have a drug in them. Chocolate, coffee, tea, and some soft drinks also contain a drug.

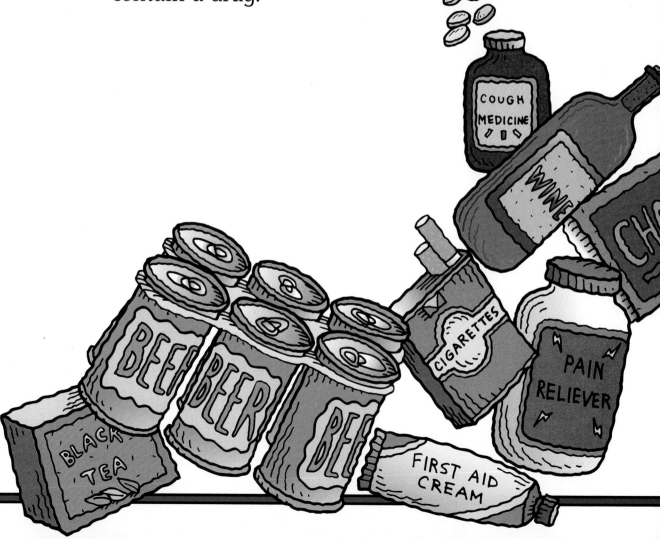

Drugs that are not medicines are not healthful for anyone, especially children. The more you learn about drugs and what they do, the easier it will be to say no to drugs.

Drugs that are medicines can help the body.

All drugs change the way the body works.

Drugs such as those in cigarettes can harm the body.

? **CHECK**

What is the difference between medicines and other drugs?

What is caffeine?

Coffee, tea, chocolate, and some soft drinks contain a drug. The drug is called **caffeine**.

Caffeine changes the way the body works. Caffeine can make the heart work harder than it should. Caffeine speeds up the body in other ways, too.

▼ **Which of these foods and drinks do you think contain caffeine? How could you find out?**

Many people drink coffee, tea, or cola drinks because the caffeine makes them feel wide awake. But too much caffeine can make people feel nervous. Sometimes using too much caffeine makes it hard to fall asleep at night.

If you want to know whether a food or drink has caffeine, read the label. Watch for caffeine, coffee, tea, or chocolate in the ingredients list.

CHECK

What does caffeine do to the body?

How can tobacco hurt the body?

Cigarettes, cigars, chewing tobacco, and pipe tobacco are all made from the **tobacco** plant. Tobacco contains a drug called **nicotine**.

Nicotine can weaken the heart by making it beat faster and work harder than it should. Nicotine and other drugs in tobacco can also cause lung disease and cancer.

It is against the law for children to use tobacco. Using tobacco in any form can hurt the body. Even breathing someone else's **tobacco smoke** is harmful.

A **habit** is something a person does over and over. The habit of using tobacco can hurt a person. People who have this habit need lots of help to stop using tobacco. The best way to avoid the habit of using tobacco is never to start.

?

CHECK
....
Name two ways using tobacco can hurt the body.

How can alcohol hurt the body?

Beer, wine, and liquor are drinks that contain alcohol. **Alcohol** is a drug. Alcohol changes the way the body works.

When a person drinks something that has alcohol, the alcohol goes to the person's brain. Alcohol makes it difficult to think clearly. Alcohol speeds up some parts of the body and slows down other parts.

Too much alcohol acts like a poison. Alcohol can harm the heart, the stomach, and the liver.

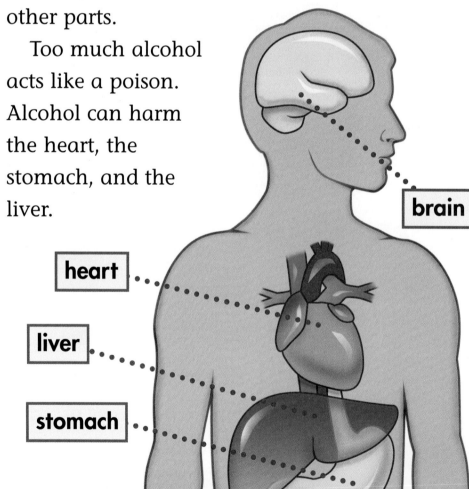

brain

heart

liver

stomach

It is against the law for children or teenagers to drink alcohol. It is also against the law for adults to drive when they have been drinking too much alcohol. Alcohol makes a person's vision blurry and slows a person's reactions.

Drinking alcohol can harm the body. If a person drinks alcohol and drives, others may get hurt, too.

?
CHECK

Why is it unsafe to drink alcohol and drive?

How can I refuse drugs?

Sometimes other people try to talk you into using drugs. People may dare you to try using tobacco or drinking alcohol. They may say it makes you more grown up. Anyone who does this is not your friend.

It takes courage to **refuse**, or say no to, drugs. Practicing ahead of time can help. So can knowing about the harm drugs can do.

Another way to stay safe from drugs is to stay away from drug containers such as alcohol bottles or cigarette packages. Follow the rules for staying safe around medicines, too.

When you see drug containers, walk on by! Then tell a trusted adult.

CHECK

List three ways to stay away from drugs.

SAY NO to Drugs

Cal is next door playing video games with a friend. His friend finds a beer can that has some beer left in it. Cal's friend wants him to taste the beer. Let's see how Cal refuses.

Learn This Skill

1. Say no, and tell why not.

No! We shouldn't drink alcohol.

Cal says no.

2. Think about what could happen.

We could get sick.

Cal knows alcohol can harm the body.

3. Suggest something else to do.

Let's get some juice instead.

Cal has a better idea.

4. Say no again. Walk away if you must.

Thanks. I didn't want to have to go home angry.

You're right. I don't want to get in trouble.

Cal helps his friend make a better choice.

Practice This Skill

Use the steps to help you solve this problem.

Glen is visiting his cousin. They want something to drink before they go to bed. Glen's cousin wants to share a can of soda that has caffeine. Use what you know about caffeine to help Glen refuse this choice.

Review

Use Health Words

medicines	instructions	drugs
caffeine	tobacco	nicotine
tobacco smoke	habit	alcohol
refuse		

Finish the sentences.

1. Something you do over and over is a ___.

2. People who are ill or hurt may take ___ to help them feel better.

3. Coffee, tea, chocolate, and some soft drinks contain ___.

4. All ___ change the way the body works.

5. Cigarettes are made from ___.

6. Always read the label on a medicine, and follow the ___.

7. The drug in tobacco is called ___.

8. If someone offers you a drug, you should ___, or say no.

9. Even people who don't smoke can be harmed by breathing ___.

10. The drug in beer, wine, and liquor is called ___.

Use Health Ideas

Answer the questions.

11. List three ways to use medicines safely.

12. How does tobacco harm the body?

13. Which things in this picture contain drugs?

Use Life Skills

Use what you know about refusing drugs to solve this problem.

14. An older player on your baseball team offers you some chewing tobacco. He says it is safe because you don't smoke it. What do you say?

Activities

• **On Your Own** Make up an ad for healthful snacks and drinks that don't have caffeine.

• **With a Team** Find out school rules about using alcohol and tobacco. Make a poster for each.

Chapter

8

Staying Safe

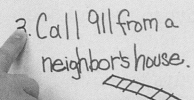

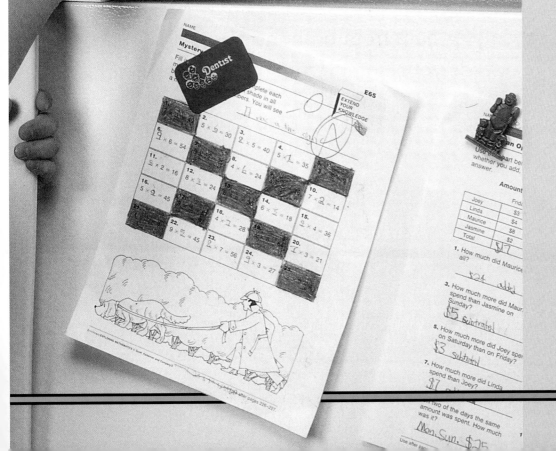

Project

Safety Posters

Use what you learn in this chapter to make safety posters. When you are finished, hang your posters at home or at school.

For more things to do, visit the Internet.
www.harcourtschool.com

How can I stay safe from fires?

The best way to stay safe from a fire is to be prepared. You practice fire drills at school. **Fire drills** help make sure everyone knows how to get out of the building safely.

Would you know what to do if a fire happened in your home?

- Know all the exits, or ways to get out of your home.
- Try to find at least two ways to leave each room.
- Pick a place for everyone to meet after leaving your home.
- Call for help from a phone outside your home.

If you get too close to a fire, your clothes may catch on fire. When this happens, you must do three things fast.

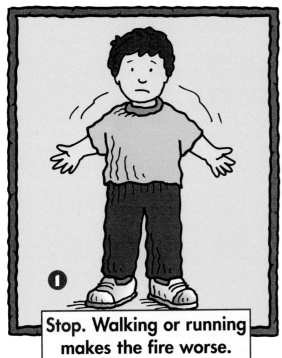

Stop. Walking or running makes the fire worse.

Drop. Fall flat on the ground.

Roll. Roll your body back and forth to put out the fire.

Fire is an emergency. You may not have time to think clearly. Practice the stop, drop, and roll so you will know what to do right away. Practice fire drills at home with your family.

?

CHECK

What should you do if your clothes catch on fire?

How can I stay safe around strangers?

A **stranger** is any person you do not know well. Some strangers are dangerous. To be safe, don't talk to strangers. Never go anywhere with a stranger.

◄ **If a stranger walks up to you, walk away quickly.**

▼ **If a stranger calls to you from a car, do not stop to talk. Do not go near the car even if the stranger asks for help. Turn and run away.**

▲ If a stranger starts talking to you in a store or a theater, tell an adult whom you trust.

▲ If a stranger comes to your home, do not answer the door. Never let a stranger into your home. Never tell a stranger that you are home alone.

If a stranger is bothering you, tell an adult or call 911 to tell the police. The numbers **911** are the telephone number to call for any emergency.

You may need to give your name, address, and telephone number if you call 911. You should know this information.

? CHECK

Name three ways to stay safe around strangers.

How can I stay safe at school?

Staying safe at school is easy when you follow your school's rules. **Rules** are made to keep you safe. You should respect the rules to keep yourself and others safe at school.

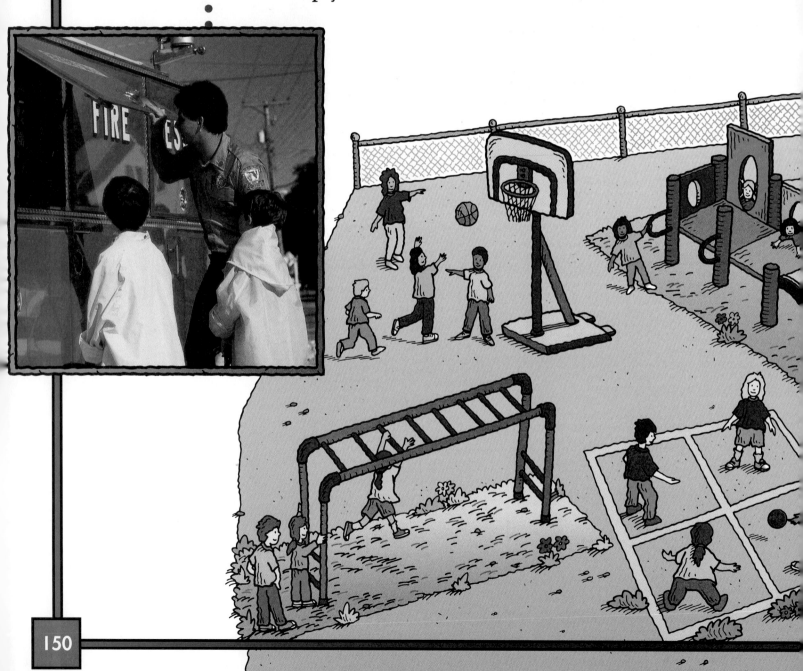

Fire drills help keep you safe at school. Firefighters may come to your school to talk about ways to stay safe from fire. Obey these fire safety rules.

Rules can also help you stay safe on the playground.

▼ Waiting your turn is one good way to stay safe on the playground. Can you name some other playground safety rules?

?
CHECK
How do rules help keep you safe at school?

RESOLVE CONFLICTS with Others

At lunchtime two teams get ready to play soccer. Nick and Monica are arguing. They both want to be the goalie for the same team. How can they resolve this conflict?

Learn This Skill

1. Agree that there is a problem.

Nick and Monica agree that neither of them is going to win this argument.

2. Listen to each other.

I'm faster. I'm stronger.

Nick and Monica agree that they each think they are the best person for that position.

3. Think of ways to work together.

How can we both play goalie?

You play for ten minutes and I'll play for ten minutes.

They agree to try to work out the problem.

4. Make the best choice.

We make a good team!

Working together is a lot better than wasting time arguing.

Practice This Skill

Use the steps to help you resolve the conflicts below.

A. Wade and his brother are fighting over whose turn it is to ride their bicycle.

B. Lee's friend Mira has a great computer game for two players. Lee wants to play, but Mira has been playing the game all week. She is tired of the computer game and wants to play a board game.

How can I stay safe outdoors?

One way to stay safe outdoors is to make sure you know how to cross the street safely.

A **crosswalk** is a marked place where you can cross a street safely. Sometimes a crossing guard helps children cross the street in a crosswalk near a school.

An **overpass** is a footbridge over a street or highway. Overpasses make it safer to cross when there is a lot of traffic.

Always follow the rules for crossing safely, even if you are at a crosswalk or on a street with no traffic.

- **Stop** before crossing the street.
- **Look** for cars or other traffic.
- **Listen** for fast-moving traffic you can't see yet.
- **Think** about what you are doing while you cross.

?
CHECK
Why should you listen before crossing the street?

How can I stay safe in a car?

The driver of a car is responsible for keeping the passengers safe. A **passenger** is someone who rides in a car or other vehicle. Passengers are also responsible for their own safety.

To stay safe, drivers and passengers must wear safety belts. A **safety belt** is a strap that keeps you safely in your seat. Everyone in the car should buckle up before the car starts.

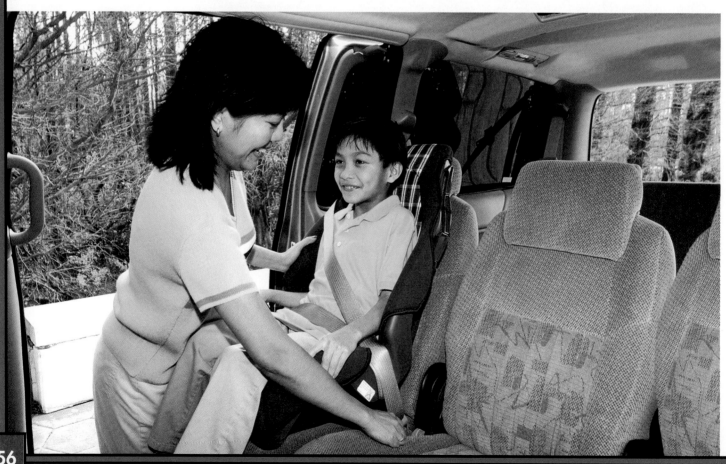

Passengers should sit quietly so the driver can pay attention to the road. Children should sit in the back seat. They should not hold or play with anything sharp or pointed while riding. Passengers should keep their heads, hands, and feet inside the car.

How are the children in the picture being responsible passengers?

?
CHECK

Why should everyone in a car wear safety belts?

How can I stay safe on a bike?

Riding a bike can be lots of fun. You can stay safe on a bike when you follow the rules.

- Wear a helmet. A **helmet** is a head covering that protects you.
- Keep both hands on the handlebars.
- Use a basket or a backpack, not your hands, if you are carrying something on your bike.

- Wear brightly colored clothing so drivers can see you.
- Always ride single file.
- Never ride without shoes. Wear shoes that protect your feet.
- Walk your bike across crosswalks.
- Obey all traffic signs.

▶ Special equipment keeps the rider safe. Tell how each thing is used.

helmet

horn

light

reflectors

? CHECK

Name two rules for riding your bike. How do these rules help keep you safe?

How can I stay safe on skates or a scooter?

Use skates, skateboards, and scooters safely to prevent injuries. An **injury** is hurt or damage to your body. When you fall or bump your body, you can get an injury.

You can stay safe when skateboarding, skating, or riding a scooter by always wearing safety gear. **Safety gear** is clothing and equipment that helps prevent injuries.

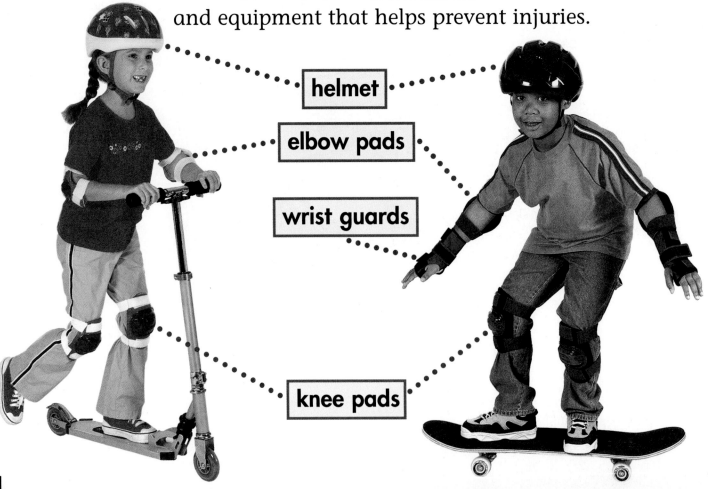

helmet

elbow pads

wrist guards

knee pads

Staying safe on skates, scooters, or skateboards means knowing how to stop. Practice stopping before you go near cars.

Also practice falling. Break your fall with your hands. Then you will not land on your back or hit your head.

Remember to skate, skateboard, or use scooters on smooth roads with no traffic. Never skate, skateboard, or ride a scooter at night. Always wear brightly colored clothing.

?
CHECK
· ·
Why should you wear safety gear when you skate, skateboard, or ride a scooter?

How can I stay safe around animals?

Many people like animals. Animals can be fun, but you have to be careful around them.

Don't make sudden moves or loud noises around an animal. Never bother an animal when it is eating or sleeping. Never tease or pull on an animal. A frightened animal may bite or scratch you.

If an animal bites you, have an adult check to see if your skin is broken. If the skin is not broken, put ice on the bite to take away the pain. If the skin is broken, wash the bite. Press a clean cloth on the bite to stop any bleeding. Call a doctor.

Tell the animal's owner about the bite. If you are bitten by a wild animal, tell an adult right away.

? CHECK

Why is it dangerous to do anything that frightens an animal?

What can I do if I get hurt?

Injuries can happen even when you try hard to stay safe. You may need emergency help when there is an injury. **First aid** is emergency help that is given right away.

First aid is needed when someone has a cut. A **cut** is a break in the skin. Cuts often bleed. You should know what to do if you or someone else gets a cut.

◀ **Put on latex gloves first if you are helping someone else. Wash the cut with soap and water.**

▶ **If the cut continues to bleed, put a clean towel over it. Press down hard. Don't stop pressing until the bleeding stops.**

◀ **If the bleeding does not stop, the cut is large, or the cut is on the face or head, get an adult's help or call 911.**

?

CHECK

What should you do when you get a cut?

Review

Use Health Words

fire drills	stranger	911	rules
crosswalk	overpass	passenger	safety belt
helmet	injury	safety gear	first aid
cut			

Finish the sentences.

1. When you skate, skateboard, or ride a scooter, you should wear proper ___.

2. To cross over a busy street or highway safely, use an ___.

3. A person who rides in a car is called a ___.

4. Protect your head from injury by wearing a ___ when you ride a bike.

5. Anyone you do not know is a ___.

6. Stay safe at school by following your school's ___.

7. In an emergency, call ___.

8. A marked place where it is safe to cross a street is called a ___.

9. A break in the skin is called a ___.

10. Even if you are careful, you might fall and get an ___.

11. To stay safe from fire, practice ___ at school and at home.

12. The help you need right away when someone is hurt is called ___.

13. Everyone in a car should wear a ___.

Use Health Ideas

Answer the questions.

14. What should you do if your clothes catch on fire?

15. Tell what the children in the picture are doing wrong. How can they ride safely?

Use Life Skills

Answer the question.

16. List four steps for resolving conflicts.

Activities

- **On Your Own** Decorate a box for your family's first-aid kit.

- **With a Team** Make a list of rules to help you stay safe at school.

Caring for My Neighborhood

Project

Neighborhood Helpers Make a guide that lists the people and groups who help your neighborhood stay healthy.

For more things to do, visit the Internet.
www.harcourtschool.com

What happens in a hospital?

A community hospital is a place people go for help to get well. What happens when someone goes to a community hospital?

Miguel's parents take him to a hospital. First Miguel gets a name bracelet. He is given a hospital gown to wear.

Then the nurse checks Miguel. The nurse asks Miguel questions about how he feels.

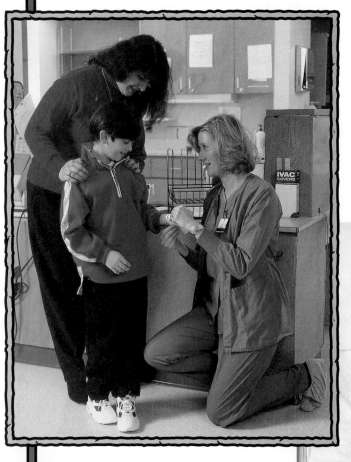

There are many ways a hospital can help. Miguel may need tests to find out what is wrong. He may need to take medicine to get well. He may need an operation to fix a health problem.

The doctors and nurses will work with Miguel's family to help him. They will answer Miguel's questions.

▶ **When Miguel leaves the hospital, he will ride in a wheelchair. Miguel can walk, but he is still weak from being in bed.**

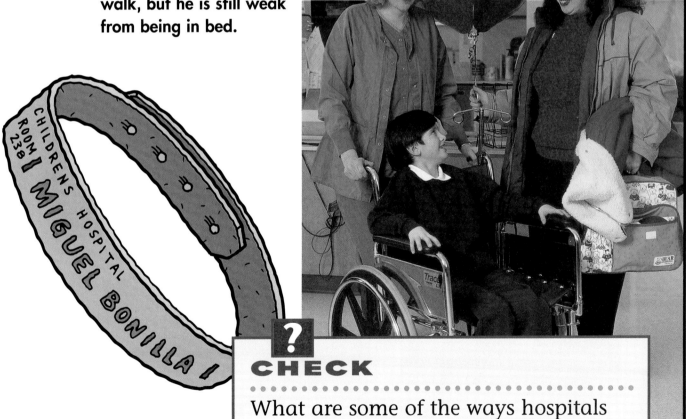

? CHECK

What are some of the ways hospitals help people who are ill?

Who works in a hospital?

All the workers in a community hospital work together to help people get well. Don't worry if you have to go to the hospital. The people who work there will take good care of you.

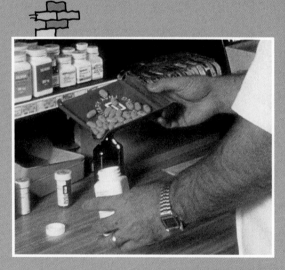

▲ This worker prepares medicines for you to take.

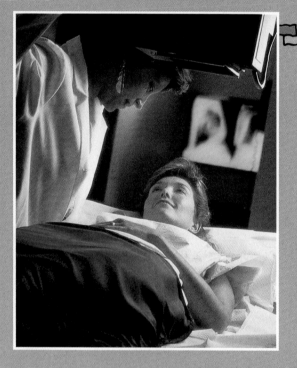

▲ This worker takes pictures of the inside of your body. These pictures are called X rays. The X rays help doctors find out what is wrong.

COMMUNITY HOSPITAL

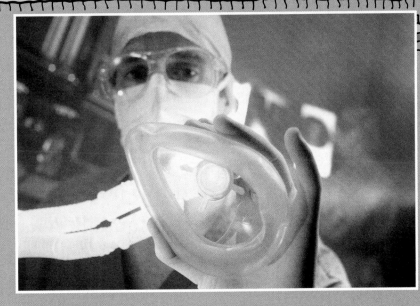

This worker helps you go to sleep before surgery. Surgery is another word for having an operation.

There are many other workers at a community hospital. Some prepare food. Others make the beds. Some clean the rooms. All these workers help the community get well and stay healthy.

? CHECK

What are some of the jobs workers do at community hospitals?

Where does the trash go?

Peach pits! Broken toys! Scribbled paper! All these things are trash. They are things people throw away.

Have you ever wondered where the trash goes after you throw it away? Your community may have a landfill. A **landfill** is a large hole in the ground that gets filled in with trash. How does trash get to the landfill? What happens when the landfill is full?

Other communities burn their trash in large furnaces, or ovens. The trash is burned until it becomes ashes. Where do you think the smoke from the burning trash goes?

? CHECK

Name two ways communities get rid of trash.

How can trash be harmful?

Having too much trash is a problem for a community. Landfills can fill up quickly. Burning trash can make lots of unhealthful smoke. If trash is just left around, it will cause disease and attract animals.

Many communities work to have less trash by recycling. **Recycling** means using things over and over instead of throwing them away.

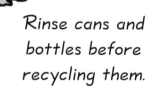

Rinse cans and bottles before recycling them.

Many kinds of trash can be recycled. Bottles, cans, and paper can all be collected and taken to recycling centers. Machines change the materials in trash into other things.

◀ This girl is using something that was made from recycled soda cans. What is it?

? CHECK

How does recycling help keep a community healthy?

MAKE DECISIONS
About Trash

Abu's class is learning about trash. He knows that some trash can be reused at home. Abu's homework is to think of a way to reuse a clean milk container. He has to choose the best way.

Learn This Skill

1. Think before you choose.

There are many ways that Abu can reuse a milk container.

2. Imagine what could happen with each choice.

Abu can use the container to make a nice gift.

3. Make the best choice.

Abu decides to make a window garden for his mother.

4. Think about what happened.

Abu's mother loved her gift. Abu felt good about recycling.

Practice This Skill

Use the steps to help you solve the problems below.

A. Think about some of the things that you throw away each day. Choose one thing, and find a way to reuse it.

B. Molly went food shopping with her father. They could buy margarine in plastic tubs or in paper wrappers. Use what you know about reusing and making decisions to help Molly and her father decide which margarine to buy.

Why is clean water important?

You need clean water to live and stay healthy. All the people, animals, and plants in your community need clean water.

Sometimes water becomes dirty. Dirt and germs in water can make people sick. Harmful things in water are known as **water pollution**.

People in your community work to keep
the water clean and free from pollution.

?
CHECK
· ·
Tell why water pollution can be a
health problem for a community.

Why is clean air important?

You need air to live. You need clean air to stay healthy.

Air pollution is dirt and other harmful things in the air. Most air pollution comes from burning. You cannot always see or smell things that pollute the air.

Air pollution can make people sick. Dirty air can harm the lungs and make it hard to breathe.

People in communities work to keep the air clean. Communities make laws to reduce smoke from cars. They make laws to keep tobacco smoke out of public places. When there is less air pollution, everyone in the community is healthier.

? CHECK

How can air pollution cause harm?

Review

Use Health Words

X rays	surgery	landfill
recycling	water pollution	air pollution

Finish the sentences.

1. In some communities trash is put in a ___.

2. Someone who is ill may need to go to a hospital for ___, or an operation.

3. Dirt and other harmful things in the air are called ___.

4. One way communities can have less trash is by ___.

5. Pictures taken of the inside of the body are called ___.

6. Harmful things in water are known as ___.

Use Health Ideas

Answer the questions.

7. What are some things that may happen if you go to a hospital?

8. How do communities fight air pollution?

9. Tell what these workers do to keep the community healthy.

Use Life Skills

Use what you know about making decisions to solve this problem.

10. Your family has a pile of old newspapers. You can throw them in the trash, take them to a recycling center, or reuse them in some way. What will you do?

Activities

- **On Your Own** Draw a picture of a healthy community.

- **With a Team** Act out a visit to a community hospital to have a broken arm fixed.

Eating Right

Getting Exercise

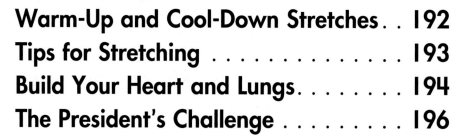

❶ Say no!

❷ Get away.

Staying Safe

③ Tell someone.

The Food Guide Pyramid

It is important to eat foods from all the food groups. The Food Guide Pyramid helps you choose healthful foods in the right amounts. You should eat more from food groups at the bottom and less from groups at the top.

Dietary Guidelines for Americans

These guidelines come from the United States Department of Agriculture (USDA). Use them to have good nutrition and to make healthful choices.

Aim for Fitness

- Try to stay at a healthy weight.
- Be physically active each day.

Build a Healthy Base

- Use the Food Guide Pyramid when you make food choices.
- Each day choose a variety of fruits, vegetables, and grains such as whole wheat and rice.
- Keep food safe to eat.

Choose Sensibly

- Choose foods with less fat and sugar.
- Choose foods with less salt. Use less added salt.

Fight Bacteria

Eating spoiled food or undercooked meat can make you ill. To keep your food safe, follow the steps shown in the picture below. And remember—when in doubt, throw it out!

FIGHT BAC!
Keep Food Safe From Bacteria ™

CLEAN Wash hands and surfaces often.

SEPARATE Don't cross-contaminate.

CHILL Refrigerate promptly.

COOK Cook to proper temperatures.

Food Safety Tips

- Wash your hands in warm, soapy water before making food. Wash your hands after making each dish.
- Keep raw meat, chicken, fish, and their juices away from other food.
- Never eat food that has raw eggs or raw egg yolks, such as cookie dough.
- After a meal, wash all dishes, knives, forks, and spoons with hot, soapy water. Also wash the tops of counters.
- Keep food that is left over in small bowls so it will cool fast. Put them in the refrigerator right away.

Getting Exercise

Warm-Up and Cool-Down Stretches

Warm up your muscles before you exercise. Spend at least five minutes stretching. You can use any of the stretches shown here. Hold each stretch while you count to 15. Repeat each stretch three times. Remember to start exercising slowly.

Slow down at the end of exercise. Then repeat some of these stretches for about two minutes. Stretching after exercise helps your muscles cool down.

▲ **Leg Stretch** Extend one leg behind you. Keep the toes of that foot pointed up.

◀ **Sit-and-Reach Stretch** Bend forward at the waist. Keep your eyes on your toes.

▼ **Upper Back and Shoulder Stretch** Try to stretch your hand down so that it rests flat against your back.

192

▶ **Thigh Stretch** Keep both hands flat on the ground. Lean as far forward as you can.

▼ **Calf Stretch** Keep both feet on the floor. Try changing the distance between your feet. Where do you get a better stretch?

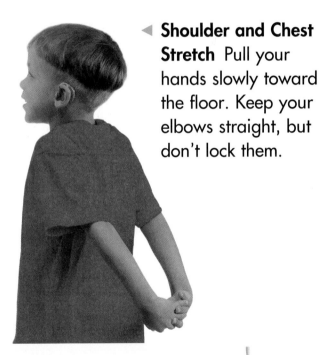

◀ **Shoulder and Chest Stretch** Pull your hands slowly toward the floor. Keep your elbows straight, but don't lock them.

Tips for Stretching

- Never bounce. Stretch gently.
- Breathe normally to get the air you need.
- Never stretch until it hurts. You should feel only a slight pull.

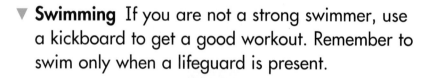
Build Your Heart and Lungs

Exercise helps your heart and lungs grow strong. The best exercise activities make you breathe deeply. They make your heart beat fast. You should try to exercise for at least twenty minutes at a time. Remember to warm up first and cool down at the end.

▲ **Skating** Always wear a helmet, elbow and knee pads, and wrist guards. Learn to skate, stop, and fall correctly.

▼ **Swimming** If you are not a strong swimmer, use a kickboard to get a good workout. Remember to swim only when a lifeguard is present.

▶ **Jumping Rope**
Jumping rope is good for your heart and your lungs. Always jump on a flat surface. Wear shoes that support your feet.

▼ **Riding a Bike** When you ride your bike, your exercise really gets you somewhere! Follow bike safety rules, and always wear your helmet.

◀ **Walking** A fast walk can help build your heart and lungs. Wear shoes that support your feet. Walk with a friend for extra fun!

195

The President's Challenge

The President's Challenge is a physical fitness program for children ages six to seventeen. There are five activities in the President's Challenge. Each activity tests the fitness of a different part of your body. Your teacher can tell you more about how to take the President's Challenge.

❶ **Curl-Ups or Sit-Ups** This exercise measures strength in the muscles below your stomach.

❷ **Shuttle Run** This exercise measures the strength of your legs. It also tests your heart and lungs.

③ One Mile Run or Walk This exercise measures the strength of your legs. It tests how long you can exercise without getting tired.

④ Pull-Ups This exercise measures strength in the muscles of your arms and shoulders.

⑤ V-Sit Reach This exercise measures how easily the muscles of your legs and back can stretch.

Fire Safety

You can stay safe from fires. Follow these safety rules.

- Never play with matches or lighters.
- Be careful around stoves, heaters, fireplaces, and grills.
- Don't use microwaves, irons, or toasters without an adult's help.
- Practice your family's emergency plan.
- If there is a fire in your home, get out quickly. Drop to the floor and crawl if the room is filled with smoke. If a closed door feels hot, don't open it. Use another exit. Call 911 from outside your home.
- If your clothes catch on fire, use Stop, Drop, and Roll right away to put out the flames.

❶ **Stop** Don't run or wave your arms.

❷ **Drop** Lie down quickly. Cover your eyes with your hands.

❸ **Roll** Roll back and forth to put out the fire.

Make a Family Emergency Plan

By having a plan, your family can protect itself during an emergency.

Know What Could Happen

Learn the possible emergencies in your area.

Have Two Meeting Places

Pick two places to meet—one a block away and one at least a mile away.

Know Your Family Contact

Choose someone who lives far away to be a contact person. Know the person's name, address, and telephone number.

Out-of-State Contact
Ms. Jane Doe
43212 Janeway Blvd.
Big City, IL 12345
(123) 555-1234

Have Emergency Drills

Practice getting out of your home safely.

Make an Emergency Kit

Gather first aid items, food, and water.

Stranger Danger

❶ Say no! Yell if you need to. You do not have to be polite to strangers.

You can stay safe around strangers. Follow these rules.

- Never talk to strangers.
- Never go with a stranger, on foot or in a car.
- If you are home alone, do not open the door. Do not let telephone callers know you are alone.
- Never give your name, address, or phone number to anyone you don't know. (You may give this information to a 911 operator in an emergency.)
- If you are lost or need help, talk to a police officer, a guard, or a store clerk.
- If a stranger bothers you, use the Stranger Danger rules to stay safe.

❷ Get away. Walk fast or run in the opposite direction. Go toward people who can help you.

❸ Tell someone. Tell a trusted adult, such as a family member, a teacher, or a police officer. Do not keep secrets about strangers.

Prevent Poisoning

A poison is something that is bad for you. It can kill you or make you very ill. Some poisons have special uses. Only adults can use them safely.

▲ These mean something is a poison.

Keep Away from Poisons

- Know the pictures and words that mark poisons.
- Never take any medicines or vitamins by yourself. Always have a trusted adult help you.
- Never use cleaning products by yourself. Never mix cleaning products.
- Never use sprays to kill insects. Always ask an adult to help you use lotions or sprays to keep insects away.

▼ Do not mix cleaners.

Safety Near Water

Water can be fun but it can harm you, too. A person can drown in five minutes or less. The best way to be safer near water is to learn how to swim.

Obey pool rules!

Water Safety Rules

- Never swim when there is no adult to watch you.
- If you cannot swim, do not use a blow-up raft to go into deep water.
- Know the rules for the beach or pool and obey them.
- Do not run or play roughly while you are near the water.
- Never dive in head-first the first time you go in the water. Go feet-first to learn how deep the water is.

POOL RULES
- No Shoving
- No Running
- Obey the Lifeguard

- Watch the weather. Get out of the water at once if you see lightning or hear thunder.
- Protect your skin with sunblock. Protect your eyes with sunglasses.
- Always wear a life jacket approved by the Coast Guard when you are in a boat.
- Know what to do in an emergency.

▲ Always wear a life jacket when you ride in a boat.

Bike Safety Check

To ride your bike safely, you need to start with a safe bike. A safe bike is the right size for you. When you sit on your bike with the pedal in the lowest position, you should be able to rest your heel on the pedal.

After checking the size of your bike, check to see that it has the right safety equipment. Your bike should have everything shown below.

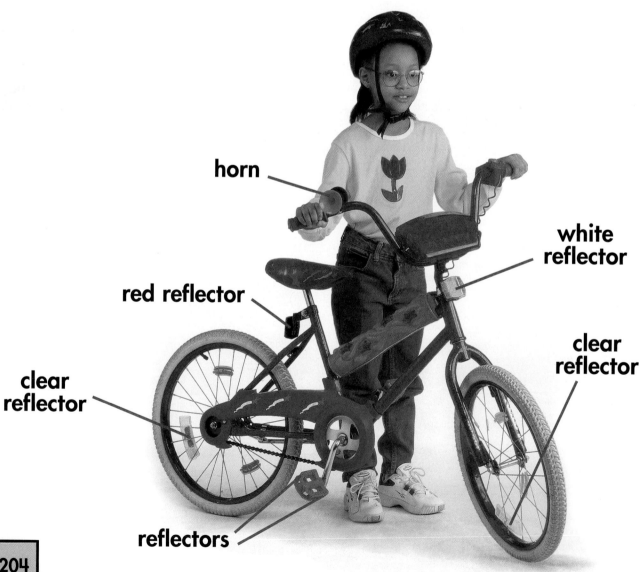

horn

white reflector

red reflector

clear reflector

clear reflector

reflectors

Your Bike Helmet

◀ **Always wear a bike helmet. Wear your helmet flat on your head. Be sure it is strapped tightly. If your helmet gets bumped in a fall, replace it right away, even if it doesn't look damaged.**

Safety While Riding

- Check your bike for safety every time you ride it.
- Ride in single file. Ride in the same direction as traffic.
- Stop, look, listen, and think when you enter a street or cross a driveway.
- Walk your bike across an intersection.
- Obey all traffic signs and signals.
- Don't ride at night without an adult. Wear light-colored clothing and use lights and reflectors for night riding.

205

Backpack Safety

Carrying a backpack that is too heavy can injure your back. Carrying one the wrong way also can hurt you.

▲ Right way

▲ Wrong way

A Safe Weight

Keep your backpack at a safe weight.

If you weigh	Your backpack should weigh no more than
45 pounds	$4\frac{1}{2}$ pounds
50 pounds	5 pounds
55 pounds	$5\frac{1}{2}$ pounds
60 pounds	6 pounds

▲ Your health book weighs a little more than $1\frac{1}{2}$ pounds.

Safe Use

- Always use both shoulder straps to carry the pack.
- Use a pack with wide shoulder straps and a padded back.

Glossary

afraid (uh•FRAYD): frightened or scared (20)

air pollution (AIR puh•LOO•shuhn): dirt and other harmful things in the air (182)

alcohol (AL•kuh•hawl): the harmful drug in beer, wine, and liquor (136)

allergy (A•ler•jee): an illness caused by the body's reaction to something (119)

apologize (uh•PAH•luh•jyz): to say sorry for doing something wrong or making a mistake (25)

arm bones (ARM BOHNZ): the bones of the arms (4)

arm muscles (ARM MUH•suhlz): the muscles that allow the arms to move (12)

asthma (AZ•muh): an illness that makes it hard to breathe (118)

blood vessels (BLUHD VEH•suhlz): the tubes of the circulatory system that carry blood through the body (8)

brain (BRAYN): the part of the nervous system that directs the way the body works (13)

caffeine (ka•FEEN): the drug in coffee, tea, chocolate, and some soft drinks (132)

calcium (KAL•see•uhm): a mineral found in some foods that helps build strong teeth and bones (60)

cavity (KA•vuh•tee): a hole in a tooth that should be filled by a dentist (64)

chores (CHAWRZ): special jobs a family member is responsible for doing to help the family (42)

circulatory system (SER•kyuh•luh•tohr•ee SIS•tuhm): the parts of the body that work together to carry blood through the body (8)

conflict (KAHN•flikt): a fight or a disagreement between people (46)

crosswalk (KRAWS•wawk): a marked place showing where to cross a street safely (154)

crown (KROWN): the part of a tooth that shows above the gum (54)

cut (KUHT): a break in the skin (165)

dentin (DEN•tin): the part of the tooth between the hard outer enamel and the soft inner pulp (55)

diaphragm (DY•uh•fram): a muscle that helps control breathing (10)

different (DIF•ruhnt): not exactly like anyone or anything else (16)

digestive system (dy•JES•tiv SIS•tuhm): the parts of the body that work together to help get energy from food (6)

disease (dih•ZEEZ): an illness (108)

drugs (DRUHGZ): things that change the way the body works (130)

eardrum (IR•druhm): the thin piece of tissue in the ear that helps a person hear (3)

enamel (ih•NA•muhl): the hard outer covering of a tooth (55)

energy (EH•ner•jee): the power the body needs to do things (90)

exercise (EK•ser•syz): active use of the body (78)

face muscles (FAYS MUH•suhlz): the muscles that help a person smile and frown (12)

family (FAM•lee): people such as parents, grandparents, sisters, and brothers (40)

fat (FAT): the part of food that contains the most energy, but that should be eaten only in small amounts (97)

feelings (FEE•lingz): ways to feel, such as happy, sad, afraid, or excited (18)

fire drills (FYR DRILZ): practice in getting out of a building safely in case of a fire (146)

first aid (FERST AYD): emergency help that is given right away when someone is hurt or ill (164)

fit (FIT): healthy and having lots of energy (78)

floss (FLAWS): special thread used to clean between the teeth (59)

Food Guide Pyramid (FOOD GYD PIR•uh•mid): a diagram that shows which food groups foods belong to and how many servings of food from each group to eat (92)

friend (FREND): someone liked and trusted who is not a family member (28)

germs (JERMZ): tiny things that can make people ill (70)

growing (GROH•ing): getting bigger and older (34)

gum (GUHM): the pink tissue in the mouth in which the teeth are rooted (54)

habit (HA•bit): something a person does over and over (135)

head lice (HED LYS): tiny bugs that live on the scalp and in the hair and are easily spread from person to person (116)

heart (HART): the muscle of the circulatory system that pumps blood through the body (8)

helmet (HEL•muht): a head covering that protects the skull and the body parts in the head (158)

hip bones (HIP BOHNZ): the bones of the hips (4)

ill (IL): not well (108)

ingredients (in•GREE•dee•uhnts): the things found in a food or the foods used in a recipe (98)

injury (INJ•ree): hurt or damage to the body (160)

inner ear (IH•ner IR): the part of the ear deepest in the head, behind the eardrum (3)

instructions (in•STRUHK•shuhnz): directions that tell how to do something, such as how to use a medicine safely (128)

iris (EYE•ruhs): the colored part of the eye (2)

landfill (LAND•fil): a large hole in the ground that gets filled in with trash and covered over with dirt (174)

leg bones (LEG BOHNZ): the bones of the legs (4)

leg muscles (LEG MUH•suhlz): the muscles that allow the legs to move (12)

love (LUHV): a special feeling of caring for someone (44)

lunch (LUHNCH): the meal most people eat in the middle of the day (96)

lungs (LUHNGZ): the parts of the respiratory system that pump air in and out of the body (10)

medicines (MEH•duh•suhnz): drugs that are used to help people feel better or stay healthy (126)

middle ear (MIH•duhl IR): the part of the ear just inside the head, separated from the inner ear by the eardrum (3)

mouth (MOWTH): the part of the digestive system that takes in food (6); a part of the respiratory system that takes in and lets out air (10)

muscular system (MUHS•kyuh•ler SIS•tuhm): the parts of the body that work together to allow movement (12)

neck muscles (NEK MUH•suhlz): the muscles used to support and turn the head (12)

nerves (NERVZ): the parts of the body that carry messages to and from the brain (13)

nervous system (NER•vuhs SIS•tuhm): the parts of the body that work together to carry messages to and from the brain and to help feel things (13)

nicotine (NIH•kuh•teen): a harmful drug found in tobacco (134)

911 (NYN WUHN WUHN): the telephone number to call when there is an emergency (149)

nose (NOHZ): a part of the respiratory system that takes in and lets out air; the part of the body that uses the sense of smell (10)

overpass (OH•ver•pas): a footbridge over a street or highway (154)

passenger (PA•suhn•jer): someone who rides in a car or other vehicle (156)

permanent teeth (PER•muh•nuhnt TEETH): the second set of teeth, which a person gets after the primary teeth fall out (57)

polite (puh•LYT): treating others nicely and with respect (27)

primary teeth (PRY•mair•ee TEETH): baby teeth; the first set of teeth a person gets (56)

pulp (PUHLP): the soft inner part of the tooth that contains a nerve (55)

pupil (PYOO•puhl): the hole in the center of the eye that opens and closes to let in light (2)

recycling (ree•SY•kling): using things over and over instead of throwing them away (176)

refuse (rih•FYOOZ): to say no to someone or something (138)

resolve (rih•ZAHLV): to solve a problem or end a conflict (46)

respect (rih•SPEKT): thoughtfulness in what is said and done (26)

respiratory system (RES•puh•ruh•tohr•ee SIS•tuhm): the parts of the body that work together to help breathing (10)

responsible (rih•SPAHNT•suh•buhl): taking care of things that should be done (38)

root (ROOT): the part of a tooth below the gum (54)

rules (ROOLZ): directions or laws to follow (150)

safety (SAYF•tee): keeping away from danger; not getting hurt (37)

safety belt (SAYF•tee BELT): a strap that keeps a person safely in the seat in a car or other vehicle (156)

safety gear (SAYF•tee GIR): clothing and equipment, such as a helmet, knee pads, elbow pads, and wrist guards, worn to prevent injuries (160)

senses (SENT•suhz): ways to use the body to learn, enjoy things, and stay safe; sight, hearing, smell, taste, and touch (36)

serving (SER•ving): the amount of a food in one helping (92)

skeletal system (SKEH•luh•tuhl SIS•tuhm): the bones; the parts of the body that support and protect softer parts (4)

skeleton (SKEH•luh•tuhn): all the bones of the body shown together (4)

skull (SKUHL): the bones of the head (5)

special (SPEH•shuhl): different from anyone or anything else (16)

spine (SPYN): the bones of the back and neck (5)

stomach (STUH•muhk): the part of the digestive system where food is broken down (6)

stomach muscles (STUH•muhk MUH•suhlz): the muscles of the stomach area (12)

stranger (STRAYN•jer): any person not known well (148)

stress (STRES): the way the body reacts to strong feelings (22)

sunburn (SUHN•bern): a burning of the skin by the sun's rays (72)

sunscreen (SUHN•skreen): a lotion or cream that protects the skin from the sun's rays (73)

surgery (SERJ•ree): an operation to help a person who is ill or injured get better (173)

teeth (TEETH): the parts of the digestive system used to bite and chew food (7)

tobacco (tuh•BA•koh): a plant containing nicotine, with leaves that are dried to make cigarettes, cigars, pipe tobacco, and chewing tobacco (134)

tobacco smoke (tuh•BA•koh SMOHK): harmful smoke, containing drugs, that comes from cigarettes, cigars, and pipes (135)

tongue (TUHNG): the part of the digestive system that helps a person taste and swallow food (7)

vaccines (vak•SEENZ): shots that keep people from getting some diseases (114)

wastes (WAYSTS): materials the body does not need (94)

water pollution (WAW•ter puh•LOO•shuhn): harmful things in water (180)

worried (WUH•reed): troubled or upset about something (20)

X rays (EKS RAYZ): pictures of the inside of the body, taken with special film (172)

Index

Boldfaced numbers refer to illustrations.